REAL PALEO
FAST & EASY

REAL PALEO

FAST & EASY

LOREN CORDAIN, PH.D.

HOUGHTON MIFFLIN HARCOURT
NEW YORK · BOSTON · 2015

For information about permission to reproduce selections from this
book, write to trade.permissions@hmhco.com or to Permissions,
Houghton Mifflin Harcourt Publishing Company, 3 Park Avenue, 19th
Floor, New York, New York 10016

www.hmhco.com

Library of Congress Cataloging-in-Publication Data is
available upon request.

ISBN 978-0-544-58264-4 (pbk); 978-0-544-58293-4 (ebk)

Book design by Waterbury Publications, Inc., Des Moines, Iowa.

Cover photography: Waterbury Publications, Inc.

Printed in The United States of America

DOC 10 9 8 7 6 5 4 3 2 1

CONTENTS

ACKNOWLEDGMENTS

Rarely do completely new paradigms of healthful eating sweep upon the world in such an overwhelming, rapid, and scientifically convincing manner as The Paleo Diet has done in the past 5 to 7 years. One of the unfortunate downsides to this worldwide popularity has been the publication of hundreds of copycat cookbooks that have inaccurately characterized and diluted the original message of my first book, *The Paleo Diet* (2002). Accordingly, these imposter cookbooks frequently embrace distinctly non-Paleo ingredients. Rest assured that all recipes, foods, and ingredients found within this cookbook fully comply with the nutritional guidelines that I have outlined in my scientific publications and which form the foundation of contemporary "Paleo Diets."

The production of any successful book, including cookbooks, requires both the direct and indirect efforts of hundreds or even thousands of talented people from all walks of life. Central to the production of this book were Ken Carlson and Lisa Kingsley, who have been essential in orchestrating the efforts of many skillful and creative people to produce the mouthwatering recipes and vibrant photos throughout this cookbook. I can't say enough about Anne Ficklen, my editor at Houghton Mifflin Harcourt, without whose support, encouragement, and literary talent this book would never have materialized. I am indebted to the multitude of scientific colleagues, students, friends, and family who have inspired me to research and write about all things "Paleo" over the past 30 years. Above all I want to acknowledge you, my dedicated Paleo audience, who "get it."

Thank you,

Loren Cordain, Ph.D.

INTRODUCTION

Our Paleo ancestors spent a good deal of time finding and processing food. When they were able to catch it or gather it, how it tasted was not particularly important. Food was about survival.

Modern-day Paleo diet followers have a very different problem. Food is abundant and readily available, which has allowed us to fill our time with other things—paid work, homemaking, education, extracurricular activities, volunteer work, social events. All of that activity doesn't allow much time for us to prepare the food we eat—even if it is easy to get. And there's another catch: We care about how it tastes. We want it to be delicious, healthy, and quick and easy to fix. That's a lot of demands on our diets.

Although things seem to be changing for the better, for decades the standard American diet has relied on highly processed convenience products that take very little time and effort to prepare. That has been their greatest—if not only—selling point. And we have paid the price for that convenience with the most precious thing we have—our health.

The modern Paleo way is about eating the basic foods our ancestors ate—unprocessed meats, poultry, fish and shellfish, eggs, nuts, lots of fresh fruits and vegetables and eliminating dairy, grains, and legumes. In a modern context, however, those are foods that require some preparation.

This presents a conundrum: Can you eat a Paleo diet and live in the modern world—with its expectation of interesting food cooked in little to no time? The answer is in the pages of this book. The recipes in this book take just 30 minutes or less from start to finish—and every one is not only delicious but also 100 percent Paleo-compliant.

How is that accomplished? Carefully chosen ingredients, smart cooking methods, and clever shortcuts—plus a boost from unadulterated convenience products that are perfectly well within the guidelines of The Paleo Diet (see pages 14 to 21). The time-saving strategy of planned-overs (recipes for a beef roast, a roasted whole chicken, a pork shoulder, and hard-cooked eggs) allow you to cook once but eat twice or more throughout the week using the leftovers in varied and delicious ways. With a little planning, Paleo Pantry items (page 292) can be prepared when you have time to spare for use any time during the week.

Can you invest 30 minutes in your health and the simple pleasure of eating real, whole food?

THE PALEO DIET: WHAT IS IT?

When I first wrote *The Paleo Diet* in 2002, it was not my intention for us to consume only the foods our hunter-gatherer ancestors ate—and in the state they ate them—but rather for us to eat only from the food groups from which they ate. That is, to eat animal proteins such as meat, poultry, fish and shellfish; fresh fruits and vegetables; and nuts and seeds—and to avoid processed foods, dairy products, grains, and legumes. There's a little more to it than that, but it's just about that simple.

THE PALEO DIET IN A NUTSHELL

- First, avoid processed foods. Focus your grocery shopping in the outside aisles of the supermarket—where the meat, poultry, fish, and fruits and vegetables are generally located—and avoid the center aisles, where packaged and processed foods are usually stocked.

- Eliminate legumes (kidney beans, lentils, lima beans, soybeans, pinto beans, navy beans, garbanzo beans, fava beans, black beans, black-eyed peas, peanuts, and so on) and grains (wheat, corn, rice, barley, rye, oats, millet, sorghum, quinoa, amaranth, etc.) because they contain certain antinutrients that are intended to discourage predation by animals, birds, and insects. These antinutrients contain toxic compounds that can impair human health.

- Eliminate dairy products. Humans are the only mammals who drink milk and eat milk products beyond infancy. A tell-tale sign that mature humans were not intended to drink milk is that 65% of all people on the planet can't consume milk or milk products without digestive distress.

- Eliminate processed sugar, honey, and added salt. The only salt you need comes from the naturally occurring salt in meat, fish, seafood, eggs, vegetables, and nuts. You will reduce your risk for high blood pressure, stroke, osteoporosis, heart disease, and many cancers. If you've been eating the standard American diet, you've been on a high-salt diet.

- Eat as many fresh fruits and nonstarchy vegetables as you like. The only exceptions to this recommendation are a few food items we think of as vegetables that are actually legumes, including sweet peas, green beans, snap peas, snow peas, alfalfa and bean sprouts, and peanuts. Dried fruits are great in moderation as long as they are unsulfured.

- Any and all animal proteins, including eggs, beef, pork, lamb, game, chicken, turkey, and all fish and shellfish, are on the Paleo menu.

- The diet Mother Nature intended is uncomplicated. There's no need to count calories or measure portions. Let your appetite be your guide. If you are eating the right foods, you will know when you feel satiated.

THE PALEO DIET AND THE 85:15 RULE

Eating Paleo does not consign you to a boring, monotonous, limited diet in any way. In fact, the deeper you get into eating this way, the better you will feel—and the more you will want to continue eating Paleo. However, from the start—when I wrote the first edition of *The Paleo Diet*—I incorporated the 85:15 Rule into the diet. The basic idea of this rule is that since most people eat about 20 meals per week, you can eat three non-Paleo meals per week—15 percent of your weekly meal total—and still experience noticeable, positive health benefits. I recommend that Paleo Diet novices begin at 85:15 for a few weeks and then steadily move toward 95:5 as they become used to the diet. (Two non-Paleo meals per week is a 90:10 compliance and one non-Paleo meal per week is a 95:5 percent compliance.) This flexible strategy allows a little bit of cheating without losing the diet's effectiveness. In fact, many Paleo dieters say that once they eliminate a former favorite food, when they do eat it, they experience unpleasant physical effects and wind up losing their cravings for that particular food..

THE PALEO DIET: THE BENEFITS

So why should you adopt The Paleo Diet? For many people, weight loss is the chief motivating factor. Many of those seeking a fit, lean body have tried low-calorie or low-fat diets to no avail—and there's a reason for that. The Paleo Diet is not a fad diet. It's a way of eating that is scientifically and evolutionarily on point. It will normalize your body weight and keep the pounds off permanently. You will not find yourself starving on The Paleo Diet. You will feel good and you will want to keep feeling good. One of the keys to its success is that in addition to lots of nutrient-packed fresh fruits and vegetables, a cornerstone of the diet is protein. All calories are not created equal. It takes two to three times more metabolic energy to turn protein into usable energy than it does with carbohydrates and fats. This means that protein boosts your metabolism and causes you to lose weight. Higher protein intake blunts appetite, so both of these effects contribute to long-term weight loss. In addition, going Paleo improves your health and well-being. You can't ward off almost every type of disease by eating in this manner. Genetic, environmental, and other factors have an impact as well. But by adhering to the basic dietary guidelines of your Paleolithic ancestors, you can reduce your risk of developing these illnesses—or improve symptoms if you are currently dealing with one of them.

THE DIET-DISEASE CONNECTION

- **Metabolic syndrome diseases.** Type 2 diabetes, heart disease, hypertension, obesity, myopia, acne, and breast, prostate, and colon cancers are all linked to insulin levels in the bloodstream. The Paleo Diet's combination of protein-rich foods with low-glycemic index fruits and vegetables encourages the normalization of blood sugar and insulin levels. Fruits and vegetables are excellent sources of antioxidants that may impede cancer, as well as phytochemicals that may be lethal to cancer cells.

- **Cardiovascular diseases.** The number-one killer in the United States is cardiovascular disease—deaths from heart attacks, stroke, high blood pressure, and other illness of the heart and blood vessels. On The Paleo Diet, your risk for cardiovascular disease will be reduced as you eat omega-3 fats found in fatty fish and monounsaturated fats found in nuts, olive oil, and avocados, and reduce or eliminate added salt, trans fats, refined sugars, grains, and high omega-6 vegetable oils while increasing fruits and veggies.

- **Osteoporosis.** People who ingest a lot of salt excrete more calcium in their urine than those who avoid salt. This leaching of calcium contributes to bone loss and osteoporosis. The Paleo Diet—which is absent of added salt—protects against this loss and increases protein intake, which stimulates bone growth.

- **Asthma.** Excess salt isn't just bad for your bones. It can also aggravate chronic asthma or exercise-induced asthma. Studies in both humans and animals have shown that salt can constrict the muscles around the small airways in the lungs.

- **Digestive diseases.** It should come as no surprise that what you eat has a strong bearing on your digestive health. Diets that include gluten-containing grains, milk, dairy, legumes, and processed foods may upset normal bowel function and promote or exacerbate digestive diseases. Studies of contemporary Paleo diets devoid of these foods have shown them to improve symptoms of irritable bowel syndrome, Crohn's disease, and ulcerative colitis.

- **Inflammatory diseases.** Illnesses that end in "itis," such as rheumatoid arthritis, ulcerative colitis, and gingivitis, can be calmed by eating omega-3 fats, which appear to have anti-inflammatory properties.

- **Autoimmune diseases.** Some diseases—such as rheumatoid arthritis, multiple sclerosis, and type 1 (juvenile) diabetes—develop when the body's immune system can't differentiate between its own tissues and those of a foreign invader. Cereal grains, dairy products, and legumes are all suspected in aggravating autoimmune diseases. Eliminating them can reduce the symptoms of these diseases.

THE PALEO DIET: THE SPECIFICS

Fresh foods are best. In terms of both flavor and nutritional content, there's no substitute for fresh vegetables, fruits, meat, eggs, poultry, fish, and seafood. Buying organic foods, free-range eggs, and grass-fed beef isn't a necessity—but it's certainly the ideal if you have access to these types of products and can afford them. Modern life forces some allowances, of course, but the order of preference is almost always: 1. fresh, 2. frozen, 3. dried, and 4. canned, bottled, or tinned.

VEGETABLES

Below is a partial list of Paleo-friendly vegetables (some are botanically fruits and some are considered fresh herbs). Enjoy them alone fresh and raw, lightly steamed, roasted, sautéed, and in any of the recipes in this book:

- Arame
- Artichoke
- Arugula
- Asparagus (green, purple, white)
- Avocado
- Bamboo shoots
- Beet greens
- Beets
- Bok choy
- Broccoli
- Brussels sprouts
- Burdock root
- Cabbage (green, red, savoy)
- Capers
- Carrots
- Cauliflower
- Celeriac (celery root)
- Celery
- Chayote
- Chickweed
- Chicory
- Chives
- Collard greens
- Cucumber
- Cucumber (English)
- Daikon radish
- Dandelion greens
- Dill
- Dulse
- Eggplant
- Endive
- Fennel root
- Fiddlehead
- Garlic
- Ginger
- Hearts of palm
- Horseradish
- Jerusalem artichoke
- Jicama
- Kale
- Kohlrabi
- Lamb's quarters
- Leeks
- Lemongrass
- Lettuce (all varieties)
- Lotus root
- Mushrooms (all edible varieties)
- Mustard greens
- Nori
- Onions
- Parsley
- Parsnip
- Peppers (all varieties)
- Pumpkin
- Purslane
- Radicchio
- Radish
- Rutabaga (Swedes)
- Seaweed
- Scallions
- Shallots
- Spinach
- Spinach (New Zealand)
- Squash (all varieties)
- Sweet potatoes
- Swiss chard
- Taro root
- Tomatillos
- Tomato
- Turnip greens
- Turnips
- Wakame
- Wasabi root
- Water chestnut
- Watercress
- Water spinach
- Yams
- Yarrow

NON-PALEO VEGETABLES

There are just a few starchy vegetables (or legumes considered to be vegetables) that should be avoided on the Paleo diet:

- Alfalfa sprouts
- Bean sprouts
- Corn
- Green beans
- Snow peas
- Sugar snap peas
- Sweet peas
- White potatoes

White potatoes are not allowed on the Paleo diet because they have a high glycemic index similar to refined grains that unfavorably influences blood sugar and insulin concentrations. Corn is not a vegetable at all but a grain. And green beans and all types of peas are actually legumes, not vegetables.

FRUITS

If you are generally healthy and not overweight or obese, you can eat as much fresh fruit as you'd like. Avoid canned fruits; they are usually packed in heavy syrups and have lost a lot of nutrients in the canning process. The one exception to this rule is the tomato. The tomato is actually a fruit, not a vegetable (though it is listed under vegetables on the opposite page because that's how it is most often used in culinary applications). Canned tomatoes, tomato paste, and tomato sauce are all allowed on the Paleo diet, as long as they don't have any added salt. Eat dried fruits in moderation; they can contain as much concentrated sugar as candy. The fruits below are grouped according to their sugar content. This is intended to be a general guide to the sugar content of various fruits. The fruits are listed in alphabetical order—not in the order of their sugar content.

DRIED FRUITS (very high in total sugars)

- Dates
- Dried apricots
- Dried figs
- Dried mango
- Dried papaya
- Dried pears
- Prunes
- Raisins (golden and regular)
- Zante currants

FRESH FRUITS (very high in total sugars)

- Banana
- Cherries, sweet
- Grapes
- Mango

FRESH FRUITS (high in total sugars)

- Apples
- Pineapple
- Purple passion fruit

FRESH FRUITS (moderate in total sugars)

- Apricots
- Blackberries
- Cantaloupe
- Cherries (sour)
- Honeydew melon
- Jackfruit
- Kiwifruit
- Nectarine
- Orange
- Peach
- Pear
- Pear (Bosc)
- Pear (D'Anjou)
- Plum
- Pomegranate
- Raspberries
- Tangerine
- Watermelon

FRESH FRUITS (low in total sugars)

- Blueberries
- Casaba melon
- Elderberries
- Figs
- Grapefruit (pink)
- Grapefruit (white)
- Guava
- Guava (strawberry)
- Mamey apple
- Papaya
- Starfruit
- Strawberries

FRESH FRUITS (very low in total sugars)

- Avocado (California)
- Avocado (Florida)
- Lemon
- Lime
- Tomato

NUTS AND SEEDS

Nuts are great sources of monounsaturated fats, which may help reduce blood cholesterol. But they are also concentrated sources of omega-6 fatty acids. A diet high in omega-6 fatty acids but low in omega-3 fatty acids can promote inflammatory conditions such as heart disease, cancer, and autoimmune diseases. So enjoy nuts and seeds, but don't overdo them. And be sure to take in food sources rich in omega-3 fatty acids, such as salmon, mackerel, herring, sardines, and other fatty fish. Enjoy the following nuts raw or roasted, but without salt:

- Almonds
- Betel nuts
- Brazil nuts
- Cashews
- Chestnuts
- Coconuts
- Flaxseeds
- Hazelnuts (filberts)
- Hemp seeds
- Kola nuts
- Macadamia nuts
- Pecans
- Pistachios
- Pumpkin seeds
- Sesame seeds
- Sunflower seeds
- Walnuts

THE PALEO DIET: THE SPECIFICS

SALAD AND COOKING OILS

Oils play a big part in Paleo Diet as both flavor agents and vehicles for cooking—but not all of them are created equally and not all of them are Paleo-friendly. Although our Stone Age ancestors did not have the technology to produce cooking oils, a number of oils maintain nutritional qualities that are consistent with the fat profiles found in the wild plant and animal foods they would have eaten. Below is a list of the salad and cooking oils that are approved for modern Paleo diets.

- Avocado oil
- Coconut oil
- Flaxseed oil
- Macadamia nut oil
- Olive oil (extra virgin is best)
- Walnut oil

NON-PALEO OILS

None of the oils listed below should be used in modern Paleo diets because they contain high concentrations of omega-6 fats (linoleic acid), antinutrients, and other unfavorable compounds. To top it off, they simply don't taste as good as the six Paleo-approved oils.

- Canola
- Corn
- Cottonseed
- Peanut
- Safflower
- Sesame
- Soybean
- Sunflower seed
- Wheat germ

FRESH MEATS AND POULTRY

One of the keys to the success of The Paleo Diet is the recommendation to consume fresh animal proteins at almost every meal. Protein is far and away the most satiating of all three macronutrients (fat, carbohydrate, and protein). When you consume these satisfying high-quality proteins at nearly every meal, your appetite will naturally regulate and you will not have the desire to overeat. Protein-rich foods—in combination with low-glycemic index fresh fruits and vegetables—encourage the normalization of blood sugar and insulin levels, which further helps to normalize your appetite. When buying meats, poultry, and eggs—if you have the option—choose free-ranging, grass-fed, or pasture-produced beef, bison, pork, lamb, and poultry. These meats are almost always pricier than their feedlot and grain-produced counterparts, so check out your neighborhood farmers market to connect directly with a rancher or farmer who has grass-fed meats, poultry, or eggs for sale. By eliminating the middleperson, you can save a considerable amount of money—and if you have a freezer, buying meat in bulk by the quarter or half side can also save you a lot of cash. Jo Robinson's website (eatwild.com) is one of the best on the Web to help you find a farmer or rancher selling grass-produced animal products in your area.

FRESH FISH AND SHELLFISH

Fish, seafood, and shellfish maintain nutritional characteristics that in many ways are similar to the wild game meats and organs that were staples in our ancestors' Stone Age diets. Fish and seafood are rich sources of the beneficial omega-3 fatty acids known as EPA and DHA and are high in protein and B vitamins. You should try to include fatty fish (salmon, mackerel, herring, and sardines) about two to three times per week in your diet to obtain sufficient quantities of EPA and DHA. Avoid farm-raised fish—particularly tilapia. If possible and affordable, choose wild fish and seafood, and as with all other Paleo ingredients, the fresher, the better. Look for fish that has a mild scent and moist flesh that appears freshly cut. Don't buy fish that has a strong, fishy odor. Whole fish should have bright, bulging eyes and bright red or pink gills.

Walnut and flaxseed oils should never be used for high-heat cooking. They contain high concentrations of polyunsaturated fats (PUFA), which make them quite fragile and unstable. When heated, they are susceptible to oxidation and degradation.

NON-PALEO INGREDIENTS

Because The Paleo Diet has become so popular and has proliferated among millions of people worldwide, the interpretations of it have become adapted and the message has become diluted as hundreds of books, blogs, and websites promote a particular version of the diet. Many of these do not follow the best science that informs the modern Paleo diet. The information below corrects some of the misnomers and mistakes that have grown out of the Paleo movement. Generally, The Paleo Diet should not include the following ingredients for staples and everyday foods:

- All cereal grains (wheat, rye, barley, oats, rice, corn, millet, and sorghum) and cereal-like grains including amaranth, quinoa, chia seeds, and buckwheat
- Amalgamations of any of the ingredients on this list, which can be combined to create all kinds of modern foods that have nothing to do with our ancestral diet. This includes cookies, cakes, doughnuts, pastries, athletic bars, pancakes, "breads," wraps (with the exception of coconut wraps), and so on.
- Bacon and all other salted and/or cured meats
- Coconut sugars
- Combinations of dried fruits, nuts, vegetable oils, sea salt, and honey—often called trail mix, GORP, or snack bars
- Date sugars
- Honey
- Maple sugars and syrup
- Most refined vegetable oils (except the 6 on the approved list)
- Nut flours (coconut and almond flours can be used in moderation as a coating, but not as an element in the aforementioned baked goods)
- Raisin sugars
- Sea salt (or Himalayan salt)

NON-PALEO FOODS TO CONSUME IN MODERATION

We live in the 21st century—not in the Stone Age—and for many reasons, we are all very glad of that.

Advances in technology, education, and medicine have increased life span and quality of life over the centuries. It is impractical or impossible to consume only Stone Age foods—and frankly, we wouldn't want to. We've come up with all kinds of new foods, flavors, and cooking techniques that elevate food from mere survival to one of life's greatest pleasures. In that spirit, there are a number of modern foods that will have no detrimental effect on your health if they are consumed in moderation. People are often amazed to discover alcohol in this group.

No data suggest that Stone Age hunter-gatherers ever drank alcohol of any type. There is no doubt that alcohol abuse can impair our health, damage the liver, and increase our risk of developing many cancers. If you presently drink in moderation or take pleasure in an occasional glass of wine or beer, there's no requirement to give up this pleasure with The Paleo Diet. In fact, moderate alcohol consumption may significantly lower the risk of heart disease. The following items are non-Paleo. Enjoy them in moderation, but don't overdo:

- Beer (one 12-ounce serving). Note: Try to purchase gluten-free beers.
- Coffee
- Nuts mixed with dried fruit (no more than 4 ounces of nuts and 2 ounces of dried fruit a day, particularly if you are trying to lose weight)
- Spirits (4 ounces). Note: Stick to spirits distilled from non-gluten-containing grains (potato vodka, rum, 100% agave tequila, and brandy).
- Tea
- Wine (two 4-ounce glasses). Note: Cooking wines frequently contain salt.

QUICK CONVENIENCE PRODUCTS

On most nights, most of us don't have much time to spend in the kitchen, but we still want to stick to Paleo principles. The convenience products on this list are all Paleo-compliant—and all are used in this book. These products help you with prep work so that even on the busiest weeknights, dinner can be interesting and different than it was last night. Good taste and variety will keep you cooking and eating Paleo—and so will how good you feel.

FRESH

- Prewashed packaged salad blends
- Prewashed packaged single varieties of lettuces
- Prewashed packaged baby spinach
- Prewashed and chopped packaged kale
- Prewashed and chopped packaged collard greens
- Prewashed and chopped packaged mustard greens
- Prewashed packaged baby carrots
- Packaged shredded or julienned carrots
- Packaged sliced carrots (carrot chips)
- Packaged diced butternut squash
- Packaged fresh cauliflower florets
- Packaged fresh broccoli florets
- Packaged broccoli slaw mix
- Packaged shredded cabbage-carrot coleslaw mix
- Packaged "angel hair" shredded cabbage
- Packaged shredded Brussels sprouts
- Packaged sliced mushrooms

REFRIGERATED

- Precut chicken breast for stir-fry
- Precut beef strips for stir-fry
- Precut beef for stew
- Preformed beef patties
- Premade unseasoned meat-and-vegetable kabobs
- Raw, peeled, and deveined shrimp
- Cooked, peeled, and deveined shrimp
- Cooked packaged crabmeat
- Precooked packaged beets
- Pomegranate seeds (arils)
- Unsweetened salt-free almond milk
- Unsweetened salt-free coconut milk

FROZEN

- Chopped green sweet pepper
- Chopped onion
- Chopped sweet pepper and onion blend
- Mirepoix blend (onion, carrot, celery)
- Diced sweet potatoes
- Diced butternut squash
- Cooked and pureed winter squash
- Chopped spinach
- Any salt- and sauce-free vegetable or vegetable blend
- Any frozen fruit
- Cooked, peeled, and deveined shrimp

CANNED

- Salt- and preservative-free chicken broth
- Salt- and preservative-free beef broth
- Salt- and preservative-free vegetable broth
- Salt- and preservative-free artichoke hearts
- Salt- and preservative-free whole tomatoes
- Salt- and preservative-free diced tomatoes
- Salt- and preservative-free fire-roasted diced tomatoes
- Salt- and preservative-free crushed tomatoes
- Salt- and preservative-free stewed tomatoes
- Salt-and preservative-free tomato paste
- Salt- and preservative-free tomato sauce
- Cooked pumpkin puree
- Salt- and preservative-free canned salmon
- Salt- and preservative-free canned tuna
- Unsweetened coconut milk

DRY GOODS

- Salt- and preservative-free coconut wraps

Just because a product comes in a package of some kind doesn't mean it has been overly processed or contains anything objectionable. Provided that the product is unadulterated—with no added salt, sugar, or other additives, it's pure Paleo.

UNSALTED
BEEF
STOCK
FOR COOKING

DICED BUTTERNUT SQUASH

NET WT 10 OZ (283g)

PACKAGE

EQUIPMENT

When you're cooking quick and easy meals, you don't need a lot of fancy equipment, but there is a baseline of a few pieces that are necessary for even the simplest cooking—and a few that are not a necessity but that are certainly nice to make meal prep extra speedy.

THE BASIC "BATTERIE"

The French term for the tools and utensils that are necessary to equip a kitchen is "batterie de cuisine." That's essentially what this list is. It assumes that you have a basic set of saucepans, skillets or sauté pans,* spoons, spatulas, scrapers, and the like. Beyond the basics, some specialized tools and equipment make cooking and eating the Paleo way much easier:

- **Baking sheets:** Large rimmed baking sheets—either 10×15 or 11×17—are indispensable for roasting vegetables, toasting nuts, and baking thin pieces of fish.

- **Blender:** While most blenders will work well for most purposes, a high-performance blender is highly beneficial for the Paleo cook. The best-known brands are Vitamix and Blendtec. Their specially designed blades and high-powered motors make silky-smooth soups, sauces, nut butters, and condiments and are especially helpful for making Dijon-Style Mustard and Cashew Cream (page 304).

- **Box grater:** This four-sided grater has different surfaces on each side for coarse or fine grating, as well as slicing.

- **Cutting boards:** Wood cutting boards won't dull your knives and are safe to use as long as you scrub them with hot soapy water and rinse and dry well.

- **Extra-large skillet:** For cooking several chops or steaks at once—or for family-scaled one-dish meals that contain meat and vegetables—this pan is a must. Look for a 14-inch skillet (curved sides) or 6-quart sauté pan (straight sides).

- **Food processor:** This machine makes quick work of chopping large amounts of vegetables and is essential for making a variety of flavorful pestos (page 301).

- **Garlic press:** The perforated cup of this tool minces garlic cloves with the squeeze of the handle.

- **Knives:** High-quality cutlery is a vital component of all Paleo kitchens. Stainless-steel knives are essential for cutting, chopping, and preparing meals. A knife sharpener will keep the blades cutting efficiently.

- **Mandoline slicer:** For quickly making uniform, paper-thin slices of root vegetables, zucchini "noodles," and matchstick or julienne-cut carrots, this tool is priceless.

- **Microwave:** This appliance isn't just for reheating foods. Smartly used, it makes fragrant chutneys in a flash (page 109) or partially cooks vegetables before finishing in the oven or on the grill for an appealing crispy brown exterior.

- **Ovenproof skillet:** Quickly sear a thick steak or chop on the stove-top, then finish it off in the oven while you prepare a salad or vegetable side dish.

- **Spiralizer:** This is very much a luxury, but if you make a lot of vegetable "noodles" such as those made from zucchini, this tool does it with a few turns of a handle. It's also great for preparing quick salads and vegetable sautés.

*Note:** Do not use aluminum cookware. When foods are heated in aluminum, small amounts of the metal are absorbed into the food and, consequently, our bodies. Studies have suggested that aluminum may contribute to low-level inflammation and may affect mental- or nervous-system function.

MAKING IT FAST & EASY

My wife, Lorrie, and I have been cooking and eating Paleo since 1990. About the only people on the planet at the time who even remotely ate in this manner were the few remaining groups of hunter-gatherers. Fast-forward to 2015, and "Paleo diet" has become the most Internet-searched dietary term for the past three years running. What a difference 25 years makes. We lead busy lives and over the years have developed a number of tips and shortcuts to prepare appetizing, yet quick and easy meals and snacks. Most of these simply involve a commonsense approach to meal preparation.

THE UNIVERSAL TECHNIQUE

The first line of defense, of course, is making extra portions that can be refrigerated for later use. For example, at the beginning of the week, Lorrie hard-cooks a dozen free-range eggs and puts them in the fridge for later use. A hard-cooked egg is one of my favorite snacks, and two of them—along with juicy apples and crispy celery sticks—make a simple lunch. For a quick and easy salad, slice a few hard-cooked eggs and place the slices on top of a big bowl of prewashed and bagged spinach leaves. Add some cooked shrimp, dress with olive oil and lemon juice, and you're done. Put it in a sealed container and take it to work.

- **Eggs to the rescue.** Breakfast is one of the easiest meals to prepare. We frequently scramble up a couple of cage-free eggs and slice open a cantaloupe or any other fresh fruit that's in season. A simple veggie omelet (diced scallions, sweet peppers, and fresh spinach) cooked in olive oil frequently appears on our morning menu and represents simplicity itself.

- **Last night's dinner is this morning's breakfast.** Instead of eggs, I often enjoy a bit of last night's main dish served cold. One of my favorites is thin-sliced London broil along with seasonal fresh fruit. We eat a lot of seafood, and a cold broiled salmon steak from the previous evening's meal goes well with a big bowl of fresh berries for breakfast. Cold broiled pork chops are a healthier and salt-free alternative to bacon.

- **Prepackaged Paleo.** While The Paleo Diet and prepackaged foods may seem to be mutually exclusive, there are products available on the market that make eating Paleo easy. One of the greatest time-saving innovations is packaged precut, prewashed salad vegetables and lettuces.

These products provide you with an instant lunchtime salad and also work wonders for those who want to eat fresh veggies but don't have time to prepare them (see page 22).

- **Cook in bulk.** Just as we do with hard-cooked eggs, Lorrie will often cook a couple pounds of grass-fed ground beef and put it in the refrigerator for later use. One of my favorite lunchtime salads is a taco salad made with romaine lettuce, chopped tomatoes, sliced red onions, avocado, and ground beef, all dressed with homemade salsa.

- **Frozen is fast.** Frozen precooked seafood is one of the best ingredients to have on hand to eat Paleo on the fly. There is shrimp, of course, but you can also find shredded cooked crabmeat. Toss either into a prepackaged salad mix and dress with any of the salad dressings in this book (see page 300) and you have an instant salad.

- **Go nuts.** Nuts and seeds are great grab-and-go sources of protein. They are delicious all by themselves, or you can mix them into salads, steamed veggies, or with dried fruit. You don't want to overdo this mixture, though, because it can be high in sugars and omega-6 fats.

- **Be prepared.** Spend some time on the weekends preparing Paleo condiments, spice blends, salad dressings, and sauces. Store in tightly sealed containers in the refrigerator or freeze (such as pesto in ice cube trays, right). Throughout the week, they add flavor to Paleo meals and snacks.

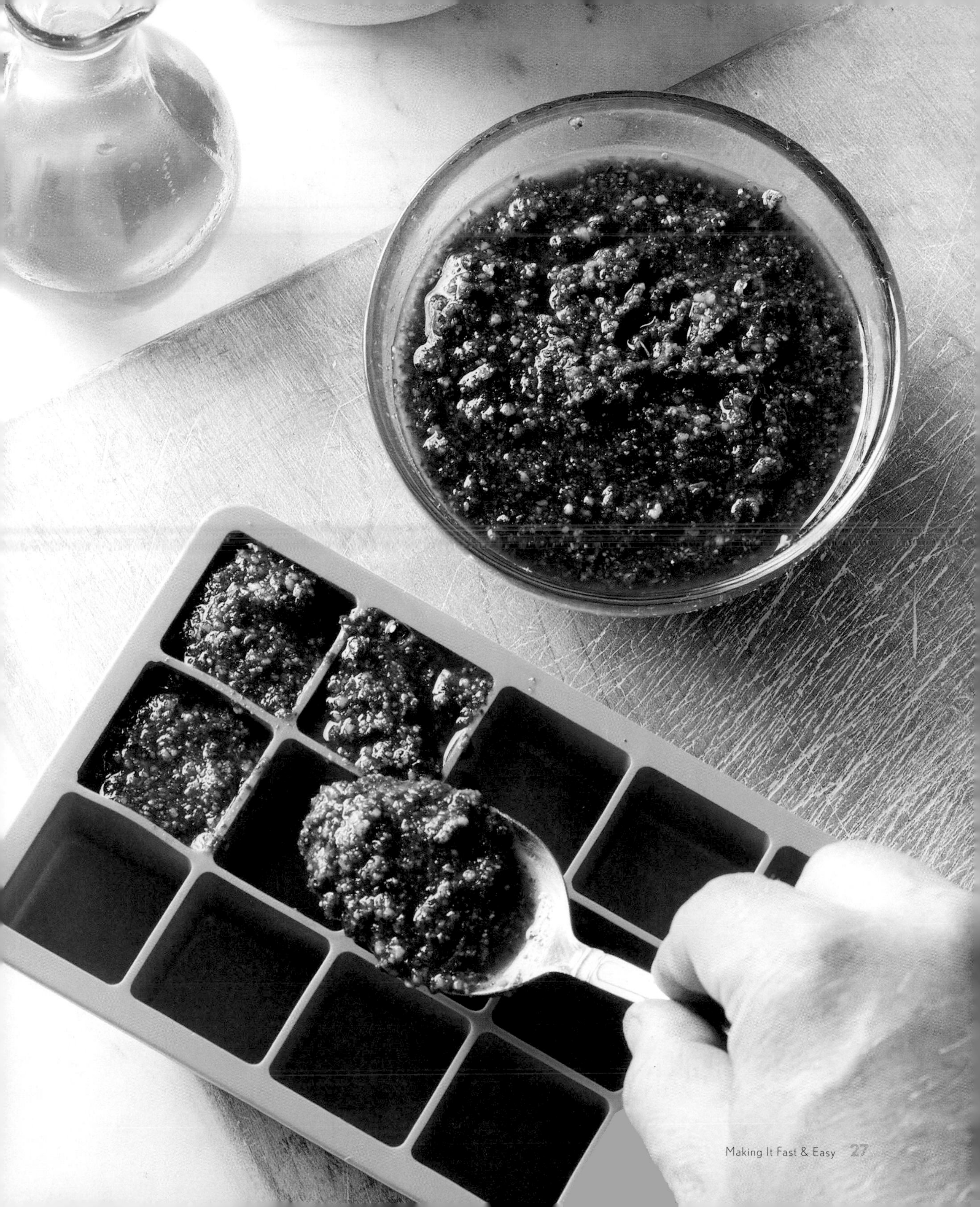

BEEF & BISON

Whether it's quick-seared steak on the grill or a speedy stir-together stew, beef and bison provide rich flavor and texture and a staying power that satisfies even the heartiest appetites. Packed with fresh vegetables, herbs, and seasonings, these delicious dishes offer great nutrition and great taste.

Meat and Potato Stew, *recipe, page 55*

CHOOSING BEEF & BISON

Certain cuts of beef and bison lend themselves more easily to quick-cooking methods—broiling, grilling, skillet-cooking, stir-frying, and high-heat roasting—than others. Obviously, size is a factor. An 8-ounce steak cooks much more quickly than a 4-pound roast. But tenderness is a factor too. Less-tender cuts of beef and bison require long, slow-moist cooking methods—great for a leisurely weekend but not for a busy weeknight.

How tender or tough a particular cut of meat is depends on where it comes from on the animal. The parts that are used for running and walking—such as the shoulder and those near the leg—are tougher. Those from the center of the animal that are not used nearly as much are more tender.

There are eight primal cuts, or "regions," on a beef animal. Starting near the head and moving back toward the tail on the top of the animal, they are the chuck, rib, short loin, sirloin, and round. Underneath the animal from front to back, they are the brisket, plate, and flank. The primal cuts on a bison are virtually identical—with the exception that the round, or back, of a beef animal is called the hip on bison.

The following are the best cuts of beef and bison for speedy dinners—as well as cooking methods for each that fit easily into a 30-minute time frame without any tenderizing or marinating time.

QUICK-COOKING CUTS

FROM THE CHUCK (SHOULDER)
- Shoulder top blade steak (flat-iron): Broil, grill, skillet-cook
- Shoulder center steak (ranch steak): Broil, grill, skillet-cook
- Shoulder petite tenders: Broil, grill, roast, skillet-cook

FROM THE SIRLOIN
- Tri-tip steak: Broil, grill, skillet-cook, stir-fry
- Top sirloin steak (boneless): Broil, grill, skillet-cook, stir-fry

FROM THE ROUND
- Top round steak: Stir-fry

FROM THE RIB
- Ribeye steak: Broil, grill, skillet-cook, stir-fry

FROM THE SHORT LOIN
- Top loin (strip) steak: Broil, grill, skillet-cook, stir-fry
- Tenderloin steak: Broil, grill, skillet-cook, stir-fry
- T-bone/porterhouse: Broil, grill, skillet-cook

FROM THE PLATE & FLANK
- Skirt steak: Stir-fry
- Flank steak: Broil, grill, stir-fry

GROUND BEEF/BISON
- Patties: Broil, grill, skillet-cook; loose meat
- Loose meat: Stir-fry, skillet-cook

BISON BASICS

There are some special considerations you might want to take when cooking bison that differ from cooking beef. Bison has far less fat than beef and dries out if overcooked. The Bison Council—a collaboration of independent American companies dedicated to producing bison products using environmentally friendly practices—recommends that you cook bison with one-third less heat for one-third less time than you would cook beef. Additionally, the color of the meat is redder than beef, so you can't rely on a visual cue to determine doneness. You will need a meat thermometer to let you know when the meat is cooked to the desired doneness. For the more tender cuts—the quick-cooking cuts featured in this book—rare or medium-rare doneness is recommended. For either beef or bison, let the meat rest for 5 to 10 minutes before cutting into it to allow the juices to be reabsorbed.

>> BASIC ROAST BEEF <<

MAKES 6 TO 8 SERVINGS

1 3- to 3½-pound boneless beef
   rump roast

3 to 4 cloves garlic, sliced
   lengthwise into halves or thirds
   (8 to 10 slivers)

1 tablespoon extra virgin olive oil
   Freshly ground black pepper

Make this roast on a Sunday evening and enjoy it with a big salad or vegetable side dish for dinner that night. Use the leftovers throughout the week to make meals that go together in a flash, including Vegetable Beef Soup (page 35), Quick Texas-Style Chili (page 37), and Italian Beef Salad (page 38).

Let roast stand at room temperature 1 hour. Preheat oven to 375°F.

Pat roast dry with paper towels. Using the tip of a sharp knife, cut 8 to 10 small incisions into roast. Tuck a sliver of garlic into each cut. Rub roast all over with olive oil and sprinkle with black pepper. Place roast on a rack in a shallow roasting pan.

Roast 30 minutes. Reduce oven temperature to 225°F. Roast an additional 1½ to 2½ hours or until a meat thermometer inserted in center of roast registers 135°F. Let roast stand 15 to 30 minutes.

To serve, thinly slice roast. To store whole roast, let cool 1 hour. Wrap tightly in a double layer of aluminum foil and store in the refrigerator up to 4 days.

>> VEGETABLE BEEF SOUP <<

MAKES 6 TO 8 SERVINGS

1 cup chopped onion

1 cup packaged julienned or
   sliced carrots

1 cup sliced celery

1 cup chopped parsnips

1 cup packaged coleslaw mix
   (shredded cabbage and carrots)

1 cup sliced fresh white or cremini
   mushrooms

1 tablespoon minced garlic (about
   6 cloves)

2 teaspoons dried thyme, crushed

2 tablespoons extra virgin olive oil

1 tablespoon no-salt-added tomato
   paste

8 cups unsalted beef stock

1 28-ounce can no-salt-added
   fire-roasted tomatoes

1 bay leaf

3 cups diced Basic Roast Beef
   (recipe, page 34)

1 tablespoon sherry or red
   wine vinegar

This warming soup only tastes like it was simmered all day. Leftover Basic Roast Beef (page 34) provides the protein, and a jumble of vegetables—carrots, celery, parsnips, shredded cabbage and carrots, mushrooms, and tomatoes—adds color and nutrition.

In a large pot cook onion, carrots, celery, parsnips, coleslaw mix, mushrooms, garlic, and thyme in hot oil over medium-high heat about 8 minutes or until onion is translucent and vegetables are crisp-tender. Stir in tomato paste; cook 1 minute or until it darkens slightly.

Add stock, undrained tomatoes, and bay leaf to pot. Bring to boiling; reduce heat. Cover and simmer 5 minutes or until vegetables are tender. Stir in beef and heat through. Stir in vinegar. Discard bay leaf.

>> QUICK TEXAS-STYLE CHILI <<

MAKES **4** SERVINGS

1 cup chopped onion

4 cloves garlic, minced

1 jalapeño chile, seeded and
   chopped*

2 tablespoons extra virgin olive oil

2 14.5-ounce cans no-salt-added
   diced tomatoes

2 cups unsalted beef stock

2 tablespoons balsamic vinegar

2 tablespoons no-salt-added
   tomato paste

2 teaspoons ground cumin

2 teaspoons smoked paprika or
   Smoky Seasoning (recipe, page
   296)

1 teaspoon dried oregano, crushed

¼ teaspoon black pepper

3 cups shredded Basic Roast Beef
   (recipe, page 34)

   Snipped fresh cilantro

   Lime wedges

   Cashew Cream (recipe, page
   304) (optional)

Smoked paprika is a magical spice. It makes this 20-minute chili taste like it was cooked all day over a smoky fire. If you like your chili with a lot of heat, leave the seeds of the jalapeño in the pepper before chopping.

In a large skillet cook onion, garlic, and jalapeño in hot oil over medium heat 5 minutes or until onion is tender. Stir in undrained tomatoes, stock, vinegar, tomato paste, cumin, paprika, oregano, and black pepper.

Add beef to skillet. Bring to boiling; reduce heat. Cover and simmer 15 minutes. Serve with cilantro, lime wedges, and, if desired, Cashew Cream.

*Tip: Chile peppers contain oils that can irritate your skin and eyes. Wear plastic or rubber gloves when working with them.

>> ITALIAN BEEF SALAD <<

MAKES **2** SERVINGS

½   cup Roasted Garlic Vinaigrette
    (recipe, page 300)

1½ teaspoons Mediterranean
    Seasoning (recipe, page 296)

1   10-ounce package Italian salad
    greens

1½ cups thinly sliced Basic Roast
    Beef (recipe, page 34)

1   8.8-ounce package refrigerated
    cooked beets, sliced

1   medium orange, peeled and
    sectioned

2   Perfectly Steamed Hard-Cooked
    Eggs, coarsely chopped (recipe,
    page 256)

¼   cup coarsely chopped toasted
    hazelnuts*

This salad is a perfect example of how a combination of planning ahead and using Paleo-approved convenience products (see page 22) makes eating Paleo on even the busiest weeknights not only possible but easy. The dressing, roast beef, and hard-cooked eggs can be made ahead with little effort. The Mediterranean Seasoning is a long-storing staple, and the packaged salad greens and refrigerated cooked beets need no preparation at all.

Whisk together Roasted Garlic Vinaigrette and Mediterranean Seasoning.

Place salad greens on a large platter or in a salad bowl. Arrange beef, beets, and orange sections on greens. Top with chopped eggs and hazelnuts. Just before serving, drizzle with vinaigrette.

*Tip: To toast hazelnuts, spread whole nuts in a shallow baking pan. Bake in a 350°F oven 5 to 10 minutes or until lightly browned, shaking pan once or twice. Watch carefully so they don't burn. Rub warm nuts in a dry dish towel until skins come loose.

STEAK WITH BUTTERNUT-BRUSSELS SPROUTS HASH

>> <<

MAKES 4 SERVINGS

4   6-ounce boneless beef top sirloin steaks, cut 1 inch thick

4   teaspoons smoked paprika

½   teaspoon black pepper

3   tablespoons coconut oil

1   pound packaged fresh butternut squash chunks

½   cup chopped onion

4   cups packaged shredded fresh Brussels sprouts

2   cloves garlic, minced

1   teaspoon ground coriander

1   teaspoon ground cumin

½   teaspoon crushed red pepper

Packaged shredded Brussels sprouts are readily available, but if your supermarket doesn't carry them, you can quickly shred whole sprouts in a food processor. Trim the sprouts, then load up the feed tube of a processor fitted with the slicing blade and just blitz them through. You'll need about 8 ounces of whole Brussels sprouts to get 4 cups of shredded sprouts.

Preheat broiler. Sprinkle both sides of steaks with 2 teaspoons of the smoked paprika and the black pepper; rub onto meat with your fingers. Place steaks on the unheated rack of a broiler pan. Broil 3 to 4 inches from heat 15 to 17 minutes for medium rare (145°F) or 20 to 22 minutes for medium (160°F), turning steaks once halfway through broiling.

Meanwhile, for hash, in an extra-large skillet heat coconut oil over medium-high heat. Add squash and onion; cook 10 to 12 minutes or just until tender, stirring occasionally. Stir in Brussels sprouts, garlic, the remaining 2 teaspoons smoked paprika, the coriander, cumin, and crushed red pepper. Cook and stir 3 to 5 minutes more or until vegetables are tender and beginning to brown.

Serve steak with hash.

GRILLED STEAK KABOBS
WITH PINEAPPLE

>>   <<

MAKES **4** SERVINGS

 1 purchased cored pineapple
 2 tablespoons salt-free garam masala
 1 tablespoon black pepper
1½ teaspoons garlic powder
 1 teaspoon coriander
 ½ teaspoon cumin
 ¼ teaspoon cayenne pepper
 8 purchased unseasoned steak and vegetable kabobs
 ½ cup extra virgin olive oil
 1 lemon, cut into wedges

The meat departments of most supermarkets carry prepared beef and chicken kabobs—especially during grilling season. Look for those that have not been marinated or seasoned in any way; they likely contain salt or other non-Paleo ingredients.

Slice pineapple into ½-inch rings. In a small bowl combine garam masala, black pepper, garlic powder, coriander, cumin, and cayenne pepper. Lightly brush the kabobs with the olive oil; sprinkle with 3 tablespoons of the seasoning mixture. Sprinkle remaining seasoning on pineapple rings.

Grill pineapple, uncovered, over medium heat 4 minutes or until grill marks appear, turning once halfway through grilling. Transfer pineapple to a serving platter. Grill kabobs, covered, 8 minutes or to desired doneness, turning once halfway through grilling. (Or cook pineapple and kabobs on a stove-top grill pan over medium heat.)

Serve kabobs with grilled pineapple and lemon wedges.

Banh Mi Beef Wraps,
recipe, page 44

>> BANH MI BEEF WRAPS <<

MAKES **4** WRAPS

½ cup coarsely shredded carrot

½ cup coarsely shredded daikon
    radish

¼ cup white wine vinegar

1 pound boneless beef top sirloin
    steak

½ teaspoon crushed red pepper

¼ cup extra virgin olive oil

4 coconut wraps

½ cup julienned English cucumber

2 small jalapeño chiles, seeded and
    cut into thin strips (tip, page 37)

½ cup fresh cilantro leaves

½ cup Paleo Mayo (recipe,
    page 305)

Lime wedges

These flavorful Vietnamese-style wraps feature an incredible combination of textures, flavors, and temperatures. Thin slices of warm, spicy beef are enveloped in a coconut wrap with a quick carrot-daikon pickle, crunchy cucumber, jalapeño, cilantro, and rich and creamy Paleo Mayo. A squeeze of fresh lime provides a finishing touch.

In a medium bowl combine carrot, daikon, and vinegar. Let stand at room temperature while preparing meat.

Thinly slice meat across the grain into bite-size strips. Sprinkle with crushed red pepper. In a large skillet heat oil over medium-high heat. Add meat to skillet; cook and stir 3 to 4 minutes or until desired doneness.

Divide meat strips among coconut wraps. Using a slotted spoon, top meat with shredded carrot and daikon; discard the liquid). Add cucumber, jalapeños, cilantro, and Paleo Mayo; roll up. Serve with lime wedges.

>> CHIMICHURRI STEAK <<

MAKES **2** SERVINGS

2 beef top loin (strip) steaks, cut
  1 inch thick

½ teaspoon black pepper

2 tablespoons extra virgin olive oil

1 medium onion, halved lengthwise
  and thinly sliced

½ teaspoon crushed red pepper

3 cloves garlic, minced

1 10-ounce package fresh
  cauliflower florets

¼ cup water

1 tablespoon fresh lemon juice

¼ cup Chimichurri Sauce (recipe,
  page 305)

Chimichurri—a beautiful, bright green Argentinian herb sauce—gives this simple steak served with spicy cauliflower gorgeous color and wonderful flavor.

Sprinkle both sides of steaks with black pepper. Grill steaks, covered, over medium heat 10 to 12 minutes for medium rare (145°F) or 12 to 15 minutes for medium (160°F), turning once halfway through grilling. (Or cook steaks on a stove-top grill pan over medium heat.)

Meanwhile, in a large skillet heat oil over medium-high heat. Add onion and crushed red pepper; cook 4 to 5 minutes or until onion softens and begins to brown. Add garlic; cook and stir 30 seconds or until fragrant. Add cauliflower and the water; cover and cook 6 to 8 minutes or just until cauliflower is tender, stirring occasionally. Uncover and cook 1 to 2 minutes more or until liquid has evaporated. Remove skillet from heat; stir in lemon juice.

Serve steaks with Chimichurri Sauce and cauliflower.

STRIP STEAK WITH
>> MUSHROOM-LEEK RELISH <<

MAKES **4** SERVINGS

¾ cup boiling water

⅓ cup dried porcini mushrooms

1 teaspoon paprika

1 teaspoon instant espresso
   coffee powder

½ teaspoon ground coriander

¾ teaspoon freshly ground black
   pepper

¼ teaspoon ground cloves

4 8-ounce beef top loin (strip)
   steaks

2 cups sliced, stemmed fresh
   shiitake mushrooms

2 medium leeks, trimmed and thinly
   sliced

3 cloves garlic, minced

2 tablespoons coconut oil

⅓ cup dry red wine

2 teaspoons snipped fresh thyme

1 10-ounce package fresh baby
   spinach

2 tablespoons water

2 tablespoons extra virgin olive oil

The reserved liquid from soaking the dried porcini mushrooms infuses the mushroom-leek relish with rich, earthy flavor. Be sure to strain the liquid well before pouring it into the pan. Porcini mushrooms harbor bits of grit that won't hurt you but don't taste great.

In a small bowl combine the boiling water and porcini mushrooms. Cover and let stand 10 to 15 minutes. In another small bowl combine paprika, espresso powder, coriander, ½ teaspoon of the pepper, and the cloves. Sprinkle spice mixture evenly over both sides of steaks; rub into meat with your fingers.

Grill steaks, covered, over medium heat 11 to 15 minutes for medium rare (145°F) or 14 to 18 minutes for medium (160°F), turning once halfway through grilling. (Or cook steaks on a stove-top grill pan over medium heat.)

Meanwhile, for mushroom-leek relish, in a large skillet cook shiitake mushrooms, leeks, and garlic in hot coconut oil over medium heat 6 to 8 minutes or until mushrooms are tender. Pour the porcini mushrooms and liquid through a fine-mesh sieve, catching the liquid in a small bowl; reserve liquid. Rinse the mushrooms with cold water; chop mushrooms. Add chopped mushrooms, the reserved liquid, the wine, thyme, and the remaining ¼ teaspoon pepper to skillet. Bring to boiling; cook, uncovered, 2 to 3 minutes or until liquid is reduced by about one-third.

Place spinach in a microwave-safe bowl; drizzle with the 2 tablespoons water. Cover and microwave 1½ to 2 minutes or just until spinach begins to wilt. Drizzle spinach with olive oil and toss to coat.

Serve steaks with mushroom-leek relish and spinach.

COFFEE-COCOA SIRLOIN STEAKS
>> WITH DRIED CHERRY-BRUSSELS <<
SPROUTS SAUTÉ

1 tablespoon unsweetened cocoa powder

1 to 1½ tablespoons finely ground coffee or espresso beans

½ teaspoon ground ancho chile pepper or chili powder

4 beef top sirloin steaks or boneless tri-tip steaks, cut ¾ inch thick (about 1¼ to 1½ pounds total)

1 to 1¼ pounds small Brussels sprouts

1 tablespoon extra virgin olive oil

½ teaspoon snipped fresh thyme

¼ teaspoon black pepper

⅓ cup unsweetened, unsulfured dried tart or sweet cherries

A combination of unsweetened cocoa, finely ground coffee, and ancho chili powder provides an aromatic and full-flavor rub for these broiled steaks. Microwaving the Brussels sprouts jump-starts the cooking process so they only need a quick pass under the broiler for a tender texture and beautiful browned exterior.

Preheat the broiler. For rub, in a small bowl stir together cocoa powder, ground coffee, and ground chile pepper. Sprinkle rub over steaks on all sides; rub into meat with your fingers.

Place steaks on the unheated rack of a broiler pan. Broil 3 to 4 inches from the heat 6 to 7 minutes for medium rare (145°F) or 8 to 9 minutes for medium (160°F). Cover and keep warm until serving time.

Meanwhile, trim stems from Brussels sprouts and remove any outer leaves. Place Brussels sprouts in a large microwave-safe bowl. Combine olive oil, thyme, and black pepper. Add to Brussels sprouts; toss to coat. Microwave, covered with vented plastic wrap, 3 to 4 minutes or until crisp-tender. Stir in dried cherries.

On a baking sheet spread Brussels sprouts and cherries in a single layer. Broil 3 to 4 inches from the heat 4 to 5 minutes or just until Brussels sprouts start to brown and are tender.

Cut steaks into thin slices. Serve with cherry-Brussels sprouts sauté.

BRANDIED RANCH STEAK WITH ARUGULA-ORANGE SALAD

>>   <<

MAKES **4** SERVINGS

- 4   6- to 8-ounce beef ranch steaks, cut 1 inch thick
- 2   teaspoons Smoky Seasoning (recipe, page 296)
- 4   tablespoons coconut oil
- 1   cup unsalted beef stock
- ½   cup finely chopped shallots
- ⅓   cup brandy
- 2   teaspoons arrowroot
- 1   tablespoon white wine vinegar
- 2   tablespoons snipped fresh chives
-   Freshly ground black pepper
- 1   recipe Arugula-Orange Salad

A salad of oranges, peppery arugula, and crunchy radishes is a refreshing side to flavorful and economical ranch steaks, which are cut from the chuck, or shoulder, of the animal. Flavored with Smoky Seasoning and pan-seared in coconut oil, they take on a beautiful brown crust. A brandy-shallot sauce provides a finishing touch.

_____

Sprinkle both sides of steaks with Smoky Seasoning. In an extra-large skillet heat 2 tablespoons of the coconut oil over medium-high heat. Add steaks. Cook 2 to 4 minutes or until well browned, turning once. Remove skillet from the heat. Carefully pour ½ cup of the stock into skillet; add shallots. Return skillet to heat. Bring to boiling; reduce heat. Cover and simmer 6 to 9 minutes for medium rare (145°F) or 9 to 12 minutes for medium (160°F). Remove steaks to a plate, reserving shallots and any pan juices in the skillet. Cover steaks to keep warm.

For pan sauce, add brandy to the skillet with shallots. Cook over medium heat 2 to 3 minutes or until liquid is reduced by about half, stirring to scrape up browned bits. In a small bowl whisk together the remaining ½ cup stock and the arrowroot until smooth; add to skillet. Whisk in vinegar. Bring to boiling. Gradually whisk in the remaining 2 tablespoons coconut oil, 1 tablespoon at a time, until combined and sauce is slightly thickened.

Spoon pan sauce over steaks; sprinkle with chives and pepper. Serve with Arugula-Orange Salad.

Arugula-Orange Salad: Divide 6 cups fresh arugula among four salad plates. Peel and section 2 oranges; remove any seeds. Top arugula with orange sections and ½ cup thinly sliced radishes. Drizzle with ⅓ to ½ cup Roasted Garlic Vinaigrette (recipe, page 300).

GRILLED STEAK AND SWEET PEPPER ROMAINE FAJITA BOATS

>> <<

MAKES **4** SERVINGS

1¼ to 1½ pounds top sirloin or flank steak, cut about ¾ inch thick

1 teaspoon cracked black pepper

½ teaspoon garlic powder

3 teaspoons extra virgin olive oil

1 large red sweet pepper, seeded and thinly sliced

1 sweet onion, thinly sliced

1 or 2 hearts of romaine lettuce

1 recipe Chimichurri Sauce (recipe, page 305)

Crunchy romaine leaves serve as vehicles for thin slices of grilled steak, peppers, and onions and a spoonful of flavorful Chimichurri Sauce.

Sprinkle steak with black pepper and garlic powder; drizzle with 2 teaspoons of the olive oil. Rub seasonings and oil into steak. Grill steak, covered, over medium heat 8 to 12 minutes or to desired doneness, turning once halfway through grilling. Remove steak from grill; let stand 5 minutes.

Meanwhile, toss sweet pepper and onion slices with the remaining 1 teaspoon olive oil. Grill over medium heat 5 minutes or until lightly charred, turning once or twice. (Or cook steaks and vegetables on a stove-top grill pan over medium-high heat.)

Thinly slice steak across the grain. Remove each leaf from the romaine heart(s). Divide sliced steak, sweet pepper, and onion among the romaine leaves. Top with Chimichurri Sauce.

>> BEEF GOULASH IN A DASH <<

2 tablespoons extra virgin olive oil

1 pound beef strips for stir-fry

8 ounces cremini mushrooms, trimmed and quartered

½ cup chopped onion

2 cloves garlic, minced

2 teaspoons sweet Hungarian paprika

½ teaspoon black pepper

1 10-ounce package frozen cubed sweet potatoes

2 cups unsalted beef stock

1 15-ounce can no-salt-added tomato sauce

½ cup Cashew Cream (recipe, page 304)

¼ cup chopped fresh parsley

1 teaspoon caraway seeds

Cashew Cream gives this Hungarian-style stew a silky texture and rich taste—you won't miss the dairy sour cream that's in the traditional version at all. It's a warming dish for a cold winter night. Serve with a crisp green salad.

In a Dutch oven or large saucepan heat 1 tablespoon of the oil over medium-high heat. Add beef; cook about 4 minutes or until browned, stirring occasionally. Remove beef to a plate.

Heat the remaining 1 tablespoon oil in the same pan. Add mushrooms, onion, and garlic; cook about 3 minutes or until softened. Sprinkle paprika and pepper over vegetables. Add sweet potatoes, stock, and tomato sauce; stir to combine. Cover and simmer 15 to 20 minutes or until potatoes are tender.

Return beef and any accumulated juices to vegetables in pan; heat through. Stir in Cashew Cream, parsley, and caraway seeds.

MOROCCAN-SPICED
>> BEEF ROULADES <<

MAKES 4 SERVINGS

- 1 10-ounce package frozen chopped spinach, thawed and squeezed dry
- ½ cup whole almonds
- ½ cup chopped dried figs
- ⅓ cup chopped fresh parsley
- ¼ cup raisins
- 1 tablespoon minced fresh ginger
- 1 teaspoon ground cinnamon
- 1 teaspoon black pepper
- ½ teaspoon coriander
- 1 to 1¼ pounds beef top round steak
- 2 tablespoons extra virgin olive oil
- 1 small onion, thinly sliced
- 2 cloves garlic, minced
- 1¼ cups unsalted beef stock
- 2 tablespoons no-salt-added tomato paste
- 6 cardamom pods, crushed
- 2 cinnamon sticks
- 2 bay leaves
- 2 tablespoons fresh lemon juice

It may not look like it, but these spinach- and dried fruit-stuffed beef rolls can actually be made in just 30 minutes. The Moroccan essence comes from the fresh ginger, cinnamon, black pepper, and coriander in the filling—and the cardamom, cinnamon, and bay in the pan sauce. They're weeknight-friendly but fancy enough for entertaining.

In a food processor combine spinach, almonds, figs, parsley, raisins, ginger, ground cinnamon, pepper, and coriander. Pulse to make a coarse paste.

Place meat on a work surface. With the notched side of a meat mallet, pound meat to about ¼-inch thickness. Spread the spinach mixture over the meat. Starting on a long side, roll up meat and tie with 100%-cotton kitchen string.

In a large skillet heat oil over medium-high heat. Sear meat in hot oil, turning meat to brown all sides. Remove meat from skillet. Add onion and garlic to the skillet; cook about 5 minutes or until onion is translucent. Stir in stock, tomato paste, cardamom pods, cinnamon sticks, bay leaves, and lemon juice. Cook about 5 minutes or until sauce is slightly thickened, stirring frequently. Return meat to the skillet. Cover and simmer gently about 5 minutes or until heated through.

Remove meat from skillet; let stand 5 to 10 minutes. Cut into ½-inch slices. Discard cardamom pods, cinnamon sticks, and bay leaves. Serve roulades with sauce.

3 WAYS WITH FIRE-ROASTED TOMATOES

It's no secret that the most primitive way of cooking—over an open fire—infuses foods with smoky flavor and attractive bits of charring. No-salt-added fire-roasted canned tomatoes are a terrific convenience product that Paleo dieters can use in all kinds of recipes for an additional flavor boost. You can roast your own tomatoes, but that isn't conducive to quick weeknight cooking. Even commercially produced fire-roasted tomatoes are simply roasted over an open fire with no added ingredients. If you like the smoky flavor of these tomatoes, you can substitute them for regular (salt-free) diced tomatoes in almost any recipe. Here are few ways to take advantage of this great product—in a hearty winter stew, a curried beef stir-fry, and a sweet and spicy beef lettuce wrap.

>> MEAT AND POTATO STEW <<

MAKES **4** SERVINGS

- 1 cup thinly sliced celery
- ½ cup chopped onion
- 1 tablespoon extra virgin olive oil
- 4 cloves garlic, minced
- 2 teaspoons paprika
- 2 teaspoons caraway seeds, crushed
- 1 teaspoon black pepper
- 4 cups unsalted beef stock
- 1 medium sweet potato, peeled and cubed
- 1 large parsnip, thinly sliced
- 1 bunch mustard greens, trimmed and coarsely torn
- 2½ cups cubed Basic Roast Beef (recipe, page 34)
- 1 14.5-ounce can no-salt-added fire-roasted diced tomatoes
- 2 teaspoons snipped fresh dill
- 2 tablespoons arrowroot
- 2 tablespoons Dijon-Style Mustard (recipe, page 304)
- 2 tablespoons cold water
- 1 tablespoon apple cider vinegar

This vibrantly colored stew is packed with nutritious vegetables—celery, sweet potato, parsnip, fire-roasted tomatoes, and mustard greens. Onion, garlic, paprika, caraway seeds, and fresh dill infuse it with flavor.

In a 4-quart Dutch oven cook celery and onion in hot oil over medium heat 5 minutes or until tender, stirring occasionally. Stir in garlic, paprika, caraway seeds, and pepper. Add stock, sweet potato, and parsnip. Bring to boiling; reduce heat. Cover and simmer 10 to 12 minutes or until vegetables are tender.

Add mustard greens and beef to pot. Return to boiling; reduce heat. Cover and simmer 3 minutes. Stir in undrained tomatoes and dill. In a small bowl stir together arrowroot, Dijon-Style Mustard, and the water until smooth. Add to stew, stirring constantly. Add vinegar. Cook and stir 2 to 3 minutes or until broth is slightly thickened.

>> CURRY-SPICED STIR-FRY <<

MAKES 4 SERVINGS

4 cups purchased fresh cauliflower florets

4 tablespoons coconut oil

1 pound boneless beef stir-fry strips

2 cups frozen chopped onion and green sweet pepper blend

½ cup purchased julienned carrots

1 to 2 fresh serrano chiles, cut into very thin strips (tip, page 37)

4 cloves garlic, minced

1 14.5-ounce can no-salt-added fire-roasted diced tomatoes

½ cup chopped fresh cilantro

1 teaspoon ground coriander

½ teaspoon saffron threads

½ teaspoon ground ginger

½ teaspoon ground cumin

¼ teaspoon ground allspice

⅔ cup unsweetened coconut milk*

Buying chopped vegetables dramatically shortens and streamlines the prep time this fragrant and spicy dish. If you can't find packaged fresh cauliflower florets in the produce section of your supermarket, pick them up from the deli's salad bar.

In a food processor pulse cauliflower (in batches if necessary) until the pieces are the size of rice. In a large skillet cook cauliflower rice in 1 tablespoon coconut oil over medium heat 5 minutes or until tender and just beginning to brown, stirring occasionally. Remove cauliflower from skillet; keep warm. Wipe out skillet.

Cut beef into thin bite-size strips. In the same skillet heat 2 tablespoons of the coconut oil over medium-high heat. Cook beef, half at a time, in the hot oil until browned, stirring occasionally. Remove beef from skillet. Drain liquid from the pan.

Add the remaining 1 tablespoon coconut oil, the onion and sweet pepper blend, carrots, serrano chile, and garlic to the skillet. Cook 5 minutes or just until vegetables are tender, stirring occasionally. Meanwhile, in the food processor pulse undrained tomatoes until smooth.

Add pureed tomatoes, ¼ cup of the cilantro, the coriander, saffron, ginger, cumin, and allspice to vegetables in skillet. Stir in the browned beef. Cook 2 to 3 minutes or until heated through, stirring frequently. Remove from heat; stir in coconut milk.

Serve stir-fry over cauliflower rice. Sprinkle with the remaining ¼ cup cilantro.

*Tip: Thoroughly mix the coconut milk before measuring to incorporate the coconut cream that rises to the top with the rest of the liquid.

SWEET AND SPICY BEEF LETTUCE WRAPS

>>   <<

MAKES 4 SERVINGS

- 1 pound ground beef
- ½ cup chopped onion
- ½ cup thinly sliced celery
- 4 cloves garlic, minced
- 1 tablespoon Cajun Seasoning (recipe, page 296)
- 1 14.5-ounce can no-salt-added fire-roasted diced tomatoes
- ⅓ cup unsweetened, unsulfured golden raisins
- ¼ cup extra virgin olive oil
- 2 tablespoons snipped fresh parsley
- 2 tablespoons fresh lemon juice
- 1 teaspoon ground cumin
- ½ teaspoon ground cinnamon
- 8 or 12 butterhead lettuce leaves
- 1 cup purchased coarsely shredded carrots

The filling in these wraps is inspired by picadillo—a favorite dish in many Spanish-speaking countries. It usually consists of ground beef or pork flavored with garlic, onions, tomatoes, cinnamon, and the sweetness of golden raisins.

In a large skillet cook beef, onion, and celery over medium heat until meat is browned. Drain off fat. Add garlic and Cajun Seasoning; cook and stir 1 minute. Add undrained tomatoes and raisins. Cook, uncovered, 3 to 5 minutes or until most of the liquid evaporates, stirring occasionally. Remove skillet from the heat; cool 5 minutes.

Meanwhile, for dressing, in a small bowl whisk together olive oil, parsley, lemon juice, cumin, and cinnamon.

Spoon meat mixture onto lettuce leaves. Top with shredded carrots and drizzle with dressing. Wrap lettuce around filling.

GINGERED BEEF STIR-FRY
>> WITH CREMINI MUSHROOMS, <<
BOK CHOY, AND TOMATOES

MAKES **4** SERVINGS

This veggie-packed stir-fry is served on a bed of angel hair shredded cabbage and is topped with roasted nuts. It has lots of color and lots of crunch.

1 orange

1½ cups unsalted beef stock

3 tablespoons minced or grated fresh ginger

1 tablespoon minced garlic (about 6 cloves)

2 teaspoons arrowroot

½ teaspoon crushed red pepper

1 pound boneless beef flank or sirloin steak

3 tablespoons extra virgin olive oil

1 small red onion, thinly sliced

4 ounces cremini mushrooms, halved

2 cups chopped baby bok choy

1 cup grape tomatoes

1 10-ounce package angel hair shredded cabbage

¼ cup chopped roasted unsalted cashews or almonds

For sauce, remove 1 tablespoon zest and squeeze ⅓ cup juice from the orange. In a large measuring cup stir together orange zest and juice, beef stock, ginger, garlic, arrowroot, and crushed red pepper.

Thinly slice meat across the grain; set aside. In a large wok or skillet heat 1 tablespoon of the oil over medium-high heat. Add the onion and mushrooms; cook and stir 2 minutes or until tender. Remove onion and mushrooms. Add 1 tablespoon of the remaining oil. Add meat to wok; cook and stir 2 minutes or until desired doneness. Remove meat. Add the remaining 1 tablespoon oil to wok; add bok choy and tomatoes. Cook and stir 1 minute or until bok choy browns slightly and tomatoes sear. Remove bok choy and tomatoes.

Return onion, mushrooms, and meat to wok; add sauce. Bring to boiling; reduce heat. Simmer, uncovered, about 2 minutes or until sauce thickens slightly. Stir in bok choy and tomatoes. Immediately serve over shredded cabbage and sprinkle with nuts.

GINGER-GARLIC FLANK
>> STEAK WITH SWEET AND TANGY << CHARRED TOMATOES

MAKES **4** SERVINGS

1   1¼- to 1½-pound beef flank steak

1   tablespoon grated fresh ginger

1   tablespoon minced garlic (about 6 cloves)

1   teaspoon freshly ground black pepper

⅔   cup balsamic vinegar

6   pitted unsweetened, unsulfured dates

2   cups cherry tomatoes

¼   of a medium red onion, cut into 1-inch chunks

2   tablespoons extra virgin olive oil

1½   cups arugula

Scoring the steak allows the rub of fresh ginger, garlic, and black pepper to penetrate the meat and infuse even the interior with flavor.

Score both sides of flank steak in a diamond pattern. Rub ginger, garlic, and pepper evenly over both sides of the steak.

Grill steak, covered, over medium heat 17 to 21 minutes for medium (160°F), turning once halfway through grilling. Remove steak from the grill; cover and let stand 5 minutes.

Meanwhile, for dressing, in a small saucepan bring vinegar and dates to boiling; reduce heat. Simmer, uncovered, 2 minutes. Remove from heat.

For the warm salad, in a large skillet cook tomatoes and onion in hot oil 6 to 8 minutes or until charred and tender, stirring occasionally. Remove skillet from heat; stir in arugula.

Thinly slice steak across the grain. Divide steak slices and warm salad among four serving plates. Spoon dressing over salad.

ARUGULA PESTO STEAK
>> WITH SQUASH, CRISPY SHALLOTS, <<
AND GOLDEN RAISINS

1 ¼   pounds beef flank steak

¼   cup Arugula Pesto (recipe,
     page 301)

4   medium shallots, thinly sliced

1   tablespoon extra virgin olive oil

2   12-ounce packages frozen
     cooked winter squash

¼   cup unsulfured golden raisins

¼   cup coarsely chopped walnuts,
     toasted*

Standing even a short time with the Arugula Pesto rubbed into it flavors the steak. While it marinates, a side dish of winter squash with savory crispy shallots and sweet raisins (it starts with frozen squash for convenience) stirs together easily.

With the notched side of a meat mallet, pound meat to ¼-inch thickness. Diagonally cut the meat across the grain into four equal pieces. Rub one side of each piece with Arugula Pesto; let stand at room temperature 15 minutes.

Meanwhile, for crispy shallots, in a medium skillet cook shallots in 1 tablespoon hot oil over medium heat 2 minutes or until golden brown; set aside. Cook squash according to package directions. Stir raisins into squash; keep warm.

Grill steak, covered, over medium heat 8 to 12 minutes for medium rare (145°F) or 12 to 15 minutes for medium (160°F), turning once halfway through grilling. (Or cook steaks on a stove-top grill pan over medium-high heat.)

Serve steak with squash; sprinkle squash with crispy shallots and walnuts.

*Tip: To toast whole or coarsely chopped nuts, spread them in a shallow baking pan. Bake in a 350°F oven 5 to 10 minutes or until toasted, shaking the pan once or twice.

>> GRILLED FLANK STEAK TACOS <<

MAKES **4** SERVINGS

1½   pounds beef flank steak

2   tablespoons salt-free chili
     powder blend

2   medium ripe avocados, seeded,
     peeled, and cubed

1   medium jalapeño chile, seeded
     and finely chopped (tip, page 37)

¼   cup chopped fresh cilantro

2   cloves garlic, minced

2   tablespoons fresh lime juice

8   to 12 large butterhead or Bibb
     lettuce leaves

1   cup chopped fresh tomato

½   cup chopped red onion

     Lime wedges (optional)

Most chili powder blends are salt-free, but read the label to be sure. You can use hot or mild chili powder—or a mix—depending on your taste.

Sprinkle both sides of steak with chili powder blend. Grill steak, covered, over medium heat 10 to 12 minutes for medium (145°F), turning once halfway through grilling. (Or cook steak on a stove-top grill pan over medium-high heat.)

Meanwhile, for guacamole, in a medium bowl combine avocados, jalapeño, cilantro, garlic, and lime juice. Mash with a potato masher or fork until chunky.

Thinly slice steak across the grain. Pile steak onto lettuce leaves. Top with guacamole, chopped tomato, and onion. If desired, serve with lime wedges.

ORANGE-SCENTED ASPARAGUS AND BEEF STIR-FRY

<<

MAKES 4 SERVINGS

2 medium oranges

2 tablespoons coconut oil

1 pound beef strips cut for stir-fry*

1 pound asparagus, trimmed and cut into 2-inch pieces

1 8-ounce package sliced shiitake mushrooms

1 sweet onion, sliced

2 teaspoons grated or minced fresh ginger

2 cloves garlic, minced

2 teaspoons arrowroot

½ cup sliced almonds, toasted (tip, page 63)

To remove the woody end of an asparagus stem, snap it off at the place where the stem easily bends—or cut about 1 inch off the bottom of the stem with a knife.

Remove 1 teaspoon zest and squeeze ⅔ cup juice from oranges; set aside.

In a wok or extra-large skillet heat 1 tablespoon of the coconut oil over high heat. Add beef; cook and stir 3 to 4 minutes or until desired doneness. Remove beef from wok.

Add the remaining 1 tablespoon coconut oil to the wok. Add asparagus, mushrooms, and onion; cook and stir 5 minutes or until crisp-tender. Add ginger and garlic; cook and stir 1 minute more.

Return beef to the wok. In a small bowl stir together the orange zest and juice and the arrowroot until smooth; stir into wok. Cook over medium heat 2 minutes or until sauce is slightly thickened. Sprinkle with almonds.

*Tip: If you can't find beef strips cut for stir-fry, use boneless beef sirloin steak and cut it into bite-size strips. Freeze the steak for 20 minutes before slicing to make the job easier.

RIBEYE STEAK WITH COCONUT CREAMED SPINACH

>>   <<

MAKES **4** SERVINGS

- 4   6- to 8-ounce boneless beef ribeye steaks, cut 1 inch thick
- 1   teaspoon cracked black pepper
- 1   15-ounce can unsweetened coconut milk
- 3   to 4 tablespoons fresh lemon juice
- 2   teaspoons arrowroot
- ⅛   to ¼ teaspoon crushed red pepper
- 1   medium shallot, thinly sliced
- 1   tablespoon coconut oil
- 2   tablespoons finely chopped fresh lemongrass or 1 tablespoon finely chopped fresh ginger
- 2   cloves garlic, minced
- 10   cups packaged fresh baby spinach
-   Lime wedges (optional)
- 1   tablespoon sesame seeds, toasted* and coarsely crushed

Classic creamed spinach is given a Paleo makeover in this recipe in which rich, velvety coconut milk stands in for the traditional cream. The coconut milk makes the spinach incredibly creamy and infuses it with wonderful flavor.

If desired, trim fat from steaks. Sprinkle steaks with pepper; press cracked black pepper into meat. Grill steaks, covered, over medium heat 11 to 15 minutes for medium rare (145°F) or 14 to 18 minutes for medium (160°F), turning once halfway through grilling. (Or cook steaks on a stove-top grill pan over medium-high heat.)

Meanwhile, for creamed spinach, in a small bowl whisk together coconut milk, lemon juice, arrowroot, and crushed red pepper until smooth; set aside. In a large skillet cook shallot in hot coconut oil over medium heat 3 to 5 minutes or just until tender, stirring occasionally. Add lemongrass and garlic; cook 1 minute. Add coconut milk mixture; cook and stir 2 to 3 minutes or until thickened. Add spinach (skillet will be full). Cook and toss about 1 minute or just until spinach is wilted.

Serve steaks with creamed spinach and, if desired, lime wedges. Sprinkle steaks with sesame seeds.

*Tip: To toast sesame seeds, scatter them in a dry skillet and toast over medium heat, stirring often so they don't burn.

HANGER STEAK WITH
>> ONION-JALAPEÑO SAUCE <<

4 tablespoons extra virgin olive oil

1 large sweet onion, thinly sliced

1 to 2 jalapeño chiles, thinly sliced
(tip, page 37)

2 cloves garlic, minced

1½ pounds hanger steak

1 cup unsalted beef stock

2 tablespoons cider vinegar

½ teaspoon Mediterranean
Seasoning (recipe, page 296)

¼ teaspoon black pepper

1 6-ounce package Kalettes*

¼ cup Classic French Vinaigrette
(recipe, page 300)

Sliced almonds, toasted (tip,
page 63) (optional)

Hanger steak has a similar flavor and texture to that of flank steak—and, in fact, comes from close to the same area of the animal. If you can't find hanger steak (sometimes called bistro steak or butcher's steak), you can substitute flank steak.

Preheat oven to 400°F. In a large skillet heat 2 tablespoons of the oil over medium-low heat. Add onion, jalapeño, and garlic. Cover and cook 13 to 15 minutes or until onion is tender, stirring occasionally. Uncover and increase heat to medium-high; cook 3 to 5 minutes or until onion is golden. Remove from heat and set aside until needed for sauce.

Meanwhile, in a large oven-going skillet heat the remaining 2 tablespoons oil over medium-high heat. Add steak; cook 4 minutes, turning once. Transfer skillet to oven. Roast, uncovered, 10 minutes or until an instant-read thermometer registers 145°F. Transfer steak to a platter; cover with foil.

For sauce, drain fat from skillet (do not wipe clean). Add ½ cup of the stock, the vinegar, Mediterranean Seasoning, and black pepper. Bring to boiling, stirring constantly to scrape up crusty browned bits from bottom of skillet. Boil gently 2 minutes. Add the onion mixture and remaining ½ cup stock to skillet; heat through.

Slice off bottoms of Kalettes and place smaller leaves in a salad bowl. Drizzle with Classic French Vinaigrette; toss to coat. Divide Kalettes among four serving plates and, if desired, sprinkle with almonds. Slice steak; add steak and sauce to plates.

*Kalettes are a cross between kale and Brussels sprouts. The flavor is savory, a bit nutty, and more subtle than that of Brussels sprouts. This non-genetically modified vegetable took 15 years to perfect and looks similar to a small cabbage.

BEFF BURGERS WITH CREAMY CUCUMBER SAUCE

>>   <<

MAKES **4** SERVINGS

2 lemons

½ cup Paleo Mayo (recipe, page 305)

¼ cup finely chopped English cucumber

½ cup chopped scallions

1½ pounds lean ground beef

1 tablespoon Mediterranean Seasoning (recipe, page 296)

1 large roma tomato, thinly sliced

8 large butterhead or Bibb lettuce leaves

A quick sauce made with Paleo Mayo, cucumber, scallions, lemon juice, and lemon zest dresses up this simple beef burger.

Preheat broiler. Remove 3 teaspoons zest and squeeze 1 teaspoon juice from the lemons.

For cucumber sauce, in a small bowl combine 1 teaspoon of the lemon zest, the lemon juice, Paleo Mayo, cucumber, and ¼ cup of the scallions. Chill until needed.

In a large bowl combine ground beef, the remaining ¼ cup scallions, the Mediterranean Seasoning, and the remaining 2 teaspoons lemon zest. Shape into four ¾-inch-thick patties.

Place patties on the unheated rack of a broiler pan. Broil 3 to 4 inches from the heat 12 to 14 minutes or until done (160°F), turning once halfway through cooking.

Top burgers with tomato slices and cucumber sauce; wrap in lettuce leaves.

SMOKY BURGERS WITH SKILLET TURNIPS AND ONIONS

>> <<

MAKES **4** SERVINGS

1 pound ground beef

4 cloves garlic, minced

1 teaspoon smoked paprika

½ teaspoon cracked black pepper

2 cups very thinly sliced turnip

1 cup thinly slivered onion

2 tablespoons coconut oil

2 teaspoons Mediterranean Seasoning (recipe, page 296)

4 tomato slices

1½ cups fresh microgreens or spring mix

¼ cup Paleo Ketchup (recipe, page 304)

This smoky burger is served with a take on the old-school side of skillet-fried potatoes and crispy onions. Sweet, thinly sliced turnips are substituted for white potatoes—which are not on the Paleo menu.

In a large bowl combine beef, garlic, paprika, and pepper. Mix well; shape into four ¾-inch-thick patties.

Grill burgers, uncovered, over medium heat 12 to 14 minutes or until done (160°F), turning once halfway through grilling. (Or cook burgers on a stove-top grill pan over medium heat.)

Meanwhile, in a large covered skillet cook turnip and onion in hot oil over medium-high heat 5 minutes, turning vegetables occasionally. Sprinkle vegetables with Mediterranean Seasoning. Toss to mix. Cook 4 to 6 minutes or just until vegetables are tender and lightly browned, turning vegetables occasionally. Reduce heat if vegetables brown too quickly.

Serve burgers on pan-fried vegetables. Top with tomato slices, microgreens, and Paleo Ketchup.

>> MILE-HIGH BURGERS <<

1 tablespoon extra virgin
   olive oil

1 large onion, thinly sliced

2 jalapeño chiles, thinly sliced
   with seeds and veins (tip,
   page 37)

2 ripe avocados, halved,
   seeded, and peeled

2 tablespoons finely chopped
   shallot

1 tablespoon fresh lime juice

¼ cup Paleo Mayo (recipe,
   page 305)

1 teaspoon Smoky Seasoning
   (recipe, page 296)

4 purchased ground beef
   patties

   Mediterranean Seasoning
   (recipe, page 296)

1 medium cucumber, chopped

¼ cup chopped shallots

1 tablespoon fresh lime juice

   Fresh dill

   Radicchio or Bibb lettuce
   leaves

"Frizzling" the onion and jalapeños in hot oil creates a little smoke and some strong aromas—but it's well worth it. The deliciously charred and spicy vegetables are a terrific combination with the rich, creamy guacamole on top of this knife-and-fork burger.

For onion-jalapeño frizzle, in a large skillet heat oil over medium heat; add onion. Cover and cook 10 minutes or until tender, stirring occasionally. Push onion to side of skillet. Add jalapeños to center of skillet; cook, uncovered, 2 to 3 minutes or until onions are golden and jalapeños are crispy. Stir onion and jalapeños together.

Meanwhile, for guacamole, in a small bowl coarsely mash avocados. Stir in the 2 tablespoons shallot and the lime juice. In another small bowl combine Paleo Mayo and Smoky Seasoning. Set aside.

Grill burgers, uncovered, over medium heat about 10 minutes or to desired doneness (145°F for medium rare or 155°F for medium), turning once halfway through grilling. (Or cook burgers on a stove-top grill pan over medium heat.) Sprinkle burgers with Mediterranean Seasoning to taste.

Meanwhile, for cucumber salad, in a small bowl combine cucumber and ¼ cup shallots. Drizzle with lime juice and sprinkle with fresh dill.

For each burger, place some of the seasoned mayo on a radicchio leaf; top with a burger, the guacamole, and onion-jalapeño frizzle. Serve with cucumber salad.

PAN-SEARED FLAT-IRON STEAK
>> WITH TOMATOES AND TOASTED <<
SPICE VINAIGRETTE

MAKES **4** SERVINGS

1½ teaspoons cumin seeds

1½ teaspoons coriander seeds

1½ teaspoons fennel seeds

⅓ cup extra virgin olive oil

3 tablespoons white wine vinegar

1½ teaspoons Dijon-Style Mustard
(recipe, page 304)

1 1-pound beef should top blade
(flat-iron) steaks

1 tablespoon extra virgin olive oil
Black pepper

4 medium heirloom or beefsteak
tomatoes, cut into ½-inch slices

1 small head butterhead lettuce,
separated into leaves

Toasting the seeds for the vinaigrette intensifies their flavor. Be sure to give the vinaigrette a good shake before drizzling it over the plate, because the crushed seeds quickly sink to the bottom of the jar.

For vinaigrette, in a small dry skillet toast cumin, coriander, and fennel seeds over medium heat about 3 minutes or until fragrant, stirring often. Cool, then lightly crush in a mortar and pestle or with the broad side of a large knife. In a screw-top jar combine crushed seeds, the ⅓ cup olive oil, the vinegar, Dijon-Style Mustard, and pepper to taste. Cover and shake until blended.

Rub steak with the 1 tablespoon olive oil; sprinkle with pepper. Grill steak, covered, over medium heat 8 to 10 minutes or to desired doneness, turning once halfway through grilling. (Or cook steak on a stove-top grill pan over medium-high heat.) Let steak stand 5 minutes.

Meanwhile, arrange lettuce on four dinner plates; top with tomato slices. Slice steak across the grain and add to plates. Shake vinaigrette and spoon over steak, tomatoes, and lettuce.

SALISBURY STEAK WITH
>> SMOTHERED ONION GRAVY <<
AND ROASTED BROCCOLI

1 bunch broccoli, cut into florets

4 tablespoons extra virgin olive oil

1 egg, lightly beaten

1½ pounds ground beef

¾ cup grated onion (grate on the big holes of a box grater and use the juice)

1 tablespoon Smoky Seasoning (recipe, page 296)

1 teaspoon dried minced rosemary

2 cups thinly sliced onions (2 large)

1 teaspoon dried thyme, crushed

1 tablespoon no-salt-added tomato paste or Paleo Ketchup (recipe, page 304)

2 teaspoons minced garlic (about 4 cloves)

¼ cup Marsala or dry sherry

2½ cups unsalted beef stock

2 teaspoons arrowroot

2 tablespoons unsalted beef stock

2 tablespoons red wine vinegar or dry sherry

Salisbury steak has always been served bun-free, so with a few adjustments, it makes a very tasty, perfectly Paleo entrée. Most gravies and sauces are thickened with cornstarch or flour, but arrowroot is used in this recipe. Arrowroot is a very fine powder made from a dried and ground tropical tuber of the same name. Arrowroot works beautifully as a thickener. It has almost twice the thickening power of wheat flour and cooks clear, so it doesn't make sauces and gravies muddy. It just needs to be mixed with a cold liquid before being added to a hot liquid.

Preheat oven to 400°F. Line two baking pans with parchment paper. Arrange broccoli on one of the pans and drizzle with 2 tablespoons of the olive oil; toss to coat.

In a large bowl combine egg, ground beef, grated onion with juice, Smoky Seasoning, and rosemary. Shape meat mixture into four ¾-inch-thick patties.

In a large skillet heat 1 tablespoon of the oil over medium-high heat. Add the patties and sear until bottoms are well browned, about 3 minutes. Carefully flip the patties over and transfer to the remaining baking pan. Roast broccoli and patties about 8 minutes or until an instant-read meat thermometer registers 140°F and broccoli is lightly charred and crisp-tender.

Meanwhile, for onion gravy, in the same skillet heat the remaining 1 tablespoon oil over medium heat. Add the onions and thyme; cook about 10 minutes or until onions are translucent, stirring occasionally. Stir in tomato paste and garlic; cook 1 minute or until tomato paste begins to darken slightly. Add Marsala; cook and stir until nearly evaporated. Add the 2 ½ cups stock and bring to a simmer. In a small bowl whisk together the arrowroot and the 2 tablespoons stock until smooth; add to skillet. Cook until sauce thickens slightly. Return the Salisbury steaks to skillet and simmer 1 minute to blend flavors. Stir in 1 tablespoon of the vinegar.

Drizzle the remaining 1 tablespoon vinegar on the broccoli. Serve Salisbury steaks with gravy and broccoli.

BEEF AND KALE
>> STUFFED MUSHROOMS <<

>> STUFFED MUSHROOMS <<

MAKES **4** SERVINGS

- 4 large fresh portobello mushrooms
- 3 tablespoons extra virgin olive oil
- ¼ teaspoon black pepper
- 1 pound lean ground beef
- ½ cup chopped onion
- ½ cup packaged shredded carrot
- 2 teaspoons dried Italian seasoning, crushed
- ½ teaspoon granulated garlic
- 2 cups packaged chopped fresh kale
- ¼ cup dried currants
- 2 tablespoons balsamic vinegar

Dried currants add a touch of sweetness to the ground beef and veggie filling for these dinner-size stuffed mushrooms.

Preheat oven to 400°F. Cut stems from mushrooms. Chop stems; set aside. Use a spoon to scrape out the gills from mushroom caps; discard gills. Brush mushrooms with 2 tablespoons of the oil; sprinkle with pepper. Place mushrooms, stem sides down, on a rimmed baking sheet. Bake 10 minutes. Turn mushrooms over. Bake 5 minutes more or until tender.

Meanwhile, in a large skillet heat the remaining 1 tablespoon oil over medium heat. Add ground beef, onion, and chopped mushroom stems; cook 5 minutes or until meat is browned. Add carrot, Italian seasoning, and garlic; cook and stir 2 to 3 minutes more or until vegetables are tender. Stir in kale and currants; cook 1 to 2 minutes or just until kale is wilted. Stir in vinegar.

Spoon ground beef filling into baked mushrooms.

PAN-ROASTED BISON
>> STEAKS AU POIVRE WITH <<
FENNEL-PARSNIP PUREE

MAKES **4** SERVINGS

2 tablespoons cracked black pepper

2 tablespoons crushed pink peppercorns

4 8-ounce bison steaks

1 tablespoon coconut oil

½ cup unsalted beef stock

¼ cup cognac or dry red wine

½ cup coconut milk*

1 recipe Fennel-Parsnip Puree

Snipped fresh tarragon or thyme (optional)

Pink peppercorns aren't really peppercorns but rather the dried berries from a type of shrub cultivated in Madagascar. Pungent and slightly sweet, they are most often found in pepper blends that include black, white, and pink peppercorns. If your supermarket doesn't have them, try a specialty spice shop. The good news is that once you've purchased them, they last for a long time.

On a large plate combine the pepper and pink peppercorns Press both sides of the bison steaks into the mixture; set aside. In a cast-iron or stainless-steel skillet heat the coconut oil over high heat just until you see wisps of smoke rising from the surface. Place bison steaks in skillet In a single layer and cook 4 minutes. Flip steaks; cook about 3 minutes more for medium rare (145°F). Remove steaks from skillet and tent with foil to keep warm.

For the sauce, reduce heat to medium. Add beef stock and cognac to hot skillet. Bring to a simmer, stirring to scrape up the browned bits from the bottom of the pan. Simmer, uncovered, about 3 minutes or until reduced by half. Stir in the coconut milk; cook about 1 minute or until thickened.

Spoon the sauce over the steaks and serve with the Fennel-Parsnip Puree. If desired, sprinkle with additional fresh tarragon or thyme.

Fennel-Parsnip Puree: In a Dutch oven heat 2 tablespoons coconut oil over medium-high heat. Add 4 parsnips, peeled and cut into 2-inch chunks; 2 fennel bulbs, trimmed and cut into 2-inch chunks; 2 leeks, halved lengthwise and cut into 2-inch pieces; and 1 clove garlic, smashed. Cook about 10 minutes or until vegetables begin to soften. Stir in 2 to 3 cups unsalted chicken stock, 2 sprigs fresh tarragon, and 2 sprigs fresh thyme. Bring to boiling; reduce heat. Cover and simmer about 15 minutes or until vegetables are tender. Transfer to a blender or food processor; pulse until smooth.

*Tip: Thoroughly mix the coconut milk before measuring to incorporate the coconut cream that rises to the top with the rest of the liquid.

JERKED PEACH AND BISON
>> BURGERS WITH GRILLED SWEET <<
POTATO AND STAR FRUIT

MAKES 4 SERVINGS

1 egg, lightly beaten

2 cloves garlic, minced

2½ teaspoons Jamaican Jerk
  Seasoning (recipe, page 296)

1 pound ground bison

½ of a ripe peach, finely chopped

1 tablespoon walnut oil or extra
  virgin olive oil

1 large sweet potato, cut into
  ¼-inch slices (at least 8 slices)

1 star fruit (carambola), cut into
  8 slices, or 8 fresh pineapple
  rings

1 recipe Paleo Aïoli (recipe,
  page 305)

A ripe peach provides a touch of sweet while Jamaican Jerk Seasoning adds a touch of heat to these lean bison burgers.

In a bowl whisk together egg, garlic, and 2 teaspoons of the Jamaican Jerk Seasoning. Add ground bison and peach; mix well. Shape into four ¾-inch-thick patties.

Grill burgers, uncovered, over medium heat about 8 to 10 minutes or until medium doneness (155°F), turning once halfway through grilling. Remove burgers; tent with foil to keep warm.

Meanwhile, soak sweet potato slices in ice water for 5 minutes. Drain and pat dry. In a large microwave-safe bowl combine oil and the remaining ½ teaspoon Jamaican Jerk Seasoning. Add sweet potatoes and toss to coat. Microwave, covered with vented plastic wrap, 4 minutes or just until tender.

Grill sweet potato and star fruit slices, uncovered, over medium heat about 5 minutes or just until heated through and grill marks appear, turning once halfway through grilling. (Or cook burgers, sweet potato, and star fruit on a stove-top grill pan over medium heat.)

Top burgers with Paleo Aïoli and serve with grilled sweet potato and star fruit.

QUICK MEAT SAUCE WITH ZUCCHINI NOODLES

>>   <<

MAKES **4** SERVINGS

- 3 tablespoons extra virgin olive oil
- 1 pound ground bison
- ½ cup chopped onion
- 3 cloves garlic, minced
- ½ cup packaged shredded carrot
- 2 teaspoons dried Italian seasoning, crushed
- 1 teaspoon Smoky Seasoning (recipe, page 296)
- 1 teaspoon crushed red pepper
- 1 28-ounce can no-salt-added crushed tomatoes
- 4 medium zucchini
- ⅓ cup chopped fresh parsley

Paleo-approved "noodles" are made from long, thin strips or spirals of vegetables—most often zucchini. If you do a lot of Paleo noodlemaking, you might consider investing in a spiralizer, a very handy kitchen tool that turns vegetables into long, beautiful noodlelike strands with a few turns of a hand crank.

For meat sauce, in a 4-quart Dutch oven heat 1 tablespoon of the olive oil over medium heat. Add ground bison, onion, and garlic; cook 5 minutes or until meat is browned. Add carrot, Italian seasoning, Smoky Seasoning, and crushed red pepper; cook and stir 2 to 3 minutes or until vegetables are tender. Stir in undrained tomatoes. Bring to boiling, reduce heat. Simmer, uncovered, 5 to 10 minutes or until the sauce is slightly reduced.

Meanwhile, trim ends off zucchini. Using a julienne cutter, mandoline, or spiralizer, cut zucchini into long thin strips. In an extra-large skillet heat the remaining 2 tablespoons olive oil over medium-high heat. Add zucchini strips; cook and stir 2 to 3 minutes or until crisp-tender.

Top zucchini with meat sauce. Sprinkle with parsley.

BISON MEAT LOAF PATTIES WITH
CHARRED ROMAINE SALAD

MAKES **4** SERVINGS

6 tablespoons extra virgin olive oil

¼ cup finely chopped onion

¼ cup finely chopped mushrooms

¼ cup finely chopped celery

2 tablespoons finely chopped apple

2 heads romaine lettuce, halved
   lengthwise

1 cup cherry or grape tomatoes

1 egg, lightly beaten

1 clove garlic, minced

½ teaspoon Lemon-Herb Seasoning
   (recipe, page 296)

1 pound ground bison

½ cup Roasted Garlic Vinaigrette
   (recipe, page 300)

Chopped onion, mushrooms, celery, and apple give these bison patties delicious flavor, moistness, and a pleasing texture.

In a large skillet heat 2 tablespoons of the olive oil over medium heat. Add onion, mushrooms, celery, and apple; cook 5 minutes or until tender. Let cool.

Preheat a stove-top grill pan over medium heat. Lightly brush cut surfaces of lettuce halves with 1 tablespoon of the oil. Place lettuce, cut sides down, on grill pan. Cook 4 minutes or until charred and slightly wilted. Remove from pan.

Meanwhile, toss tomatoes with 1 tablespoon of the oil; set aside.

In a medium bowl combine cooled onion mixture, egg, garlic, and Lemon-Herb seasoning. Add bison and mix gently yet thoroughly. Shape into four ½-inch-thick patties. Generously coat both sides of patties and the grill pan with the remaining oil. Place patties and tomatoes on grill pan. Cook 10 minutes or to desired doneness (145°F for medium rare or 155°F for medium), turning once halfway through cooking.

Drizzle Roasted Garlic Vinaigrette over patties, romaine, and tomatoes.

Grilling directions: Prepare lettuce and patties as directed. Toss tomatoes with 1 tablespoon oil and place in a grill basket. Grill lettuce, tomatoes, and patties, covered, over medium heat.

SKILLET BISON-CREMINI
>> SHEPHERD'S PIE WITH MASHED <<
CAULIFLOWER TOPPING

MAKES 4 SERVINGS

1 pound ground bison
½ teaspoon black pepper
4 tablespoons extra virgin olive oil
1 8-ounce package sliced fresh cremini mushrooms
1 cup packaged thinly sliced carrots
½ teaspoon dried thyme, crushed
2 tomatoes, seeded and chopped
1 16-ounce package frozen cauliflower florets
3 tablespoons unsalted chicken stock
1 teaspoon garlic powder
1 teaspoon Lemon-Herb Seasoning (recipe, page 296)
½ teaspoon paprika
Fresh thyme (optional)

A quick pass under the broiler results in a beautiful crust for the mashed-cauliflower topping on this skillet shepherd's pie.

Preheat broiler. Sprinkle bison with pepper. In a large oven-going skillet heat 1 tablespoon of the oil over medium-high heat. Add bison to skillet; cook until browned. Add mushrooms, carrots, and thyme. Cook 8 minutes more or just until vegetables are tender. Stir in tomatoes. Cook 2 minutes more or just until tomatoes soften. Remove skillet from heat.

Meanwhile, in a microwave-safe bowl combine cauliflower and stock. Microwave, covered, for 8 minutes or until tender. Drain well. Add 2 tablespoons of the olive oil, garlic powder, and the Lemon-Herb Seasoning to the drained cauliflower. Using a potato masher, mash cauliflower. Spread mashed cauliflower over the meat mixture; drizzle with the remaining 1 tablespoon olive oil. Sprinkle with paprika.

Broil 4 to 5 inches from the heat 3 to 5 minutes or until top is lightly browned. If desired, top with fresh thyme.

PORK & LAMB

Although pork is generally mild in flavor and lamb has a richer taste, both are widely available as quick-cooking chops and ground meat—and both lend themselves to all sorts of flavor profiles. Pork takes beautifully to Mexican, Latin American, Asian, and Southern dishes while lamb is very much at home with Mediterranean preparations and Middle Eastern flavors.

Smashed Garlic-Sage Chops with
Zucchini Noodles, recipe, page 111

CHOOSING PORK & LAMB

As with beef and bison, certain cuts of pork and lamb lend themselves more easily to quick-cooking methods—broiling, grilling, skillet-cooking, and high-heat roasting—than others. And, as with beef and bison, size obviously has a bearing on how long a cut needs to cook. Tenderness is a factor too. Less-tender cuts of pork and lamb require long, slow, moist cooking methods—which are not conducive to busy weeknight cooking.

The tenderness or toughness of a particular cut of pork or lamb depends on its source on the animal. The parts that are used for running and walking—such as the shoulder and those near the leg—are tougher. Those from the center of the animal that are not used nearly as much are more tender.

Although they vary a bit from butcher to butcher, there are essentially four primal cuts, or regions, on a pig—the shoulder, the loin (the back), the side or belly, and the leg or ham. On a lamb, there are five primal cuts—the shoulder, rib, loin, leg, and foreshank and breast.

The following are the best cuts of pork for speedy dinners—as well as cooking methods for each that fit easily into a 30-minute time frame (to a safe temperature of 145°F for steaks and chops and 160°F for patties) without any tenderizing or marinating time. There are only a few quick-cooking cuts on lamb—essentially two types of chops. See the "Lamb Basics," opposite, for more details.

QUICK-COOKING CUTS OF PORK

FROM THE SHOULDER
- **Blade steak:** Broil, grill, skillet-cook

FROM THE LOIN
- **Top loin chop:** Broil, grill, skillet-cook
- **Butterfly chop:** Broil, grill, skillet-cook

- **Boneless sirloin chop:** Broil, grill, skillet-cook
- **Loin chop:** Broil, grill, skillet-cook
- **Country-style ribs:** Broil
- **Sirloin chop:** Broil, grill, skillet-cook
- **Rib chop:** Broil, grill, skillet-cook
- **Tenderloin:** Grill, roast

LAMB BASICS

Lamb is a very tasty, often overlooked protein. This maybe because it is not always readily available at all supermarkets—and because it is pricier than other meats. If you can afford it, the rich, meaty taste of lamb is well worth it. Surprisingly, most cuts of lamb come from areas of the animal that require long, slow cooking—in particular, the leg and shank. The most popular cuts of lamb for quick cooking are two types of chops—the rib chop and the loin chop. The rib chop is cut from the rib roast—what's known as a rack of lamb. The petite bones are often "Frenched," which means the meat and membrane have been scraped away for an attractive presentation. The other type of chop is the loin chop. It is the lamb's answer to a Porterhouse steak. It's thicker and meatier than a lamb rib chop, with a T-bone in the center—similar to that of a beef T-bone steak. Either type of chop—rib or loin—can be grilled, broiled, roasted, or skillet-cooked in less than 30 minutes.

>> BASIC BRAISED PORK SHOULDER <<

MAKES ABOUT **10** CUPS
SHREDDED MEAT

1 4- to 6-pound boneless pork shoulder roast or one 5- to 7-pound bone-in pork shoulder roast

2 tablespoons desired seasoning blend (recipes, page 296)

2 teaspoons black pepper

1 tablespoon extra virgin olive oil

1 large yellow onion, sliced

4 cloves garlic, smashed

1½ cups unsalted chicken stock, dry white or red wine, or orange juice

This tender, juicy pork shoulder roast can be done unattended in the slow cooker or on the weekend for use during the week. Enjoy it on its own or in Roasted Acorn Squash with Spiced Elderberry Shredded pork (page 93), Mexican Pork Wraps with Mango-Lime Broccoli Slaw (page 95), Brazilian Pork Shoulder with Sofrito Greens (page 96), or Cuban Pork Wraps with Quick Pickles (page 97)— all of which take 30 minutes or less to make.

Adjust oven rack to lower third of oven; preheat oven to 325°F. Trim any large pieces of fat from roast. Cut boneless roast into several fist-size pieces. (Leave bone-in roast whole.) Sprinkle meat with desired seasoning blend and pepper; rub into meat.

In a Dutch oven heat oil over medium-high heat. Add meat to Dutch oven; brown on all sides, working in batches if necessary to avoid crowding pan. Nestle onion and garlic alongside pork in Dutch oven. Pour stock over meat. Bring to simmering over medium-high heat.

Cover pot and bake 2 hours or until meat is very tender. (If meat is not done after 2 hours, begin checking for doneness every 30 minutes. Cooking time will vary depending on size of roast and presence or absence of bone. The bone-in roast will take longer to cook.)

Transfer meat to a large bowl, leaving liquid in the Dutch oven. When cool enough to handle, use two forks or your hands to shred the meat. Discard bones and large pieces of fat. Strain the cooking liquid. Mix some of the liquid into the pork to moisten.

Use immediately or store in airtight containers up to 4 days in the refrigerator or freeze up to 3 months.

Slow Cooker Method: Prepare meat as directed, browning meat if desired. Place meat in a 5- to 6-quart slow cooker; add onion, garlic, and stock. Cover and cook on low setting 8 to 10 hours or high setting 5 to 6 hours. Continue as directed.

ROASTED ACORN SQUASH
>> WITH SPICED ELDERBERRY <<
SHREDDED PORK

MAKES 4 SERVINGS

2 small acorn squash (about
   1½ pounds each)
2¼ cups hot water
¾ cup unsweetened, unsulfured
   dried black elderberries
½ cup balsamic vinegar
1 1-inch piece fresh ginger, cut into
   thin coins
1 teaspoon ground cinnamon
3 tablespoons coconut oil, melted
½ teaspoon black pepper
¼ cup minced shallot
2 cloves garlic, minced
3 cups shredded Basic Braised Pork
   Shoulder (recipe, page 92)
¼ cup snipped fresh parsley

Elderberries are an immune-boosting fruit that have a rich, winelike flavor. Research also suggests that they help reduce joint inflammation.

Preheat oven to 425°F. Cut squash in half lengthwise. Scoop out seeds and strings. Place squash halves, cut sides down, on a large microwave-safe plate. Microwave, uncovered, 8 to 10 minutes or until nearly tender.

Meanwhile, in a large saucepan combine the hot water, elderberries, vinegar, ginger, and cinnamon. Bring to boiling; reduce heat to maintain a gentle boil. Cook, uncovered, 10 to 15 minutes or until reduced to about 1 cup, whisking occasionally.

In a 13×9×2-inch baking pan place the squash halves, cut sides up. Brush with 2 tablespoons of the melted coconut oil and sprinkle with pepper. Roast, uncovered, 5 to 10 minutes or until tender and lightly browned.

Pour elderberry mixture through a fine-mesh sieve into a 4-cup glass measuring cup; press the berries to extract all the juice. Discard solids. Measure ¼ cup of the liquid and set aside.

In the same large saucepan cook shallot and garlic in the remaining 1 tablespoon coconut oil over medium heat for 30 seconds. Return the remaining elderberry liquid to the saucepan; stir in shredded pork. Cook for 2 to 3 minutes or until heated through, stirring frequently.

Place squash halves, cut sides up, on serving plates. Spoon pork into squash halves. Drizzle with the reserved ¼ cup elderberry liquid and sprinkle with parsley.

MEXICAN PORK WRAPS WITH
MANGO-LIME BROCCOLI SLAW

>> <<

MAKES 4 WRAPS

2 cups packaged broccoli slaw mix

½ cup chopped cucumber

½ cup snipped fresh cilantro

¼ cup thinly sliced radishes

¼ cup Mango-Lime Salad Dressing (recipe, page 300)

1 jalapeño chile, seeded and finely chopped (tip, page 37)

1 tablespoon extra virgin olive oil

1¼ cups coarsely chopped Basic Braised Pork Shoulder (recipe, page 92)

1 tablespoon Mexican Seasoning (recipe, page 296)

4 coconut wraps

Coconut wraps are wonderful grain-free alternatives to wheat and corn tortillas and sandwich wraps. Look for coconut wraps that don't have any added ingredients, such as salt. Paleo-compliant coconut wraps are made only from pressed coconut meat, coconut water, and coconut oil.

For slaw, in a medium bowl combine broccoli slaw mix, cucumber, cilantro, and radishes. Drizzle with Mango-Lime Salad Dressing; toss to coat. Refrigerate the slaw until ready to assemble the wraps.

In a large skillet cook jalapeño in hot oil 2 minutes, stirring constantly. Add pork and Mexican Seasoning. Cook and stir 3 minutes or until heated through.

Top each coconut wrap with about ½ cup of the slaw and a generous ½ cup of the pork; roll up to enclose the fillings. Serve immediately.

BRAZILIAN PORK SHOULDER
WITH SOFRITO GREENS

>>   <<

MAKES **4** SERVINGS

5   tablespoons extra virgin olive
    oil

1   cup thinly sliced onion

3   tablespoons minced garlic

2   tablespoons Smoky
    Seasoning (recipe, page
    296)

1   bay leaf

4   cups coarsely chopped Basic
    Braised Pork Shoulder
    (recipe, page 92)

1   14.5-ounce can no-salt-
    added fire-roasted tomatoes

¾   cup unsalted chicken stock

1½ cups finely chopped onions*

1½ cups finely chopped red sweet
    peppers*

1   teaspoon crushed red pepper

2   bunches collard greens,
    trimmed and thinly sliced
    into ribbons

2   oranges, peeled and sliced
    crosswise

Sofrito refers to a mixture of ingredients—usually onions, peppers, and chiles of some type—that are chopped into small pieces and sautéed as a flavor base for many Spanish, Portuguese, and Latin American meat and vegetable dishes.

In a large skillet heat 3 tablespoons of the olive oil over medium-high heat. Add the sliced onion, 2 tablespoons of the minced garlic, the Smoky Seasoning, and bay leaf. Cook and stir 5 minutes or until onion is softened and translucent. Stir in the pork, undrained tomatoes, and stock. Bring to boiling; reduce heat. Simmer, uncovered, 10 minutes or until heated through and slightly reduced. Discard bay leaf.

Meanwhile, in another large skillet heat the remaining 2 tablespoons olive oil over medium-high heat. Add the finely chopped onions, sweet peppers, and crushed red pepper. Cook and stir 3 minutes or until fragrant. Add the collard greens; cook and toss 3 minutes or until greens are wilted.

Divide collard greens among four shallow bowls and top with the pork mixture and orange slices.

*Tip: Use a food processor to quickly chop onions and sweet peppers.

CUBAN PORK WRAP
>>   WITH QUICK PICKLES   <<

MAKES **4** SERVINGS

1 tablespoon extra virgin olive oil

1 small onion, thinly sliced

3 cloves garlic, minced

1½ cups pulled or coarsely chopped Basic Braised Pork Shoulder (recipe, page 92)

1½ teaspoons ground cumin

1½ teaspoons dried oregano, crushed

½ teaspoon crushed red pepper

3 tablespoons fresh orange juice

2 tablespoons fresh lime juice

2 tablespoons Paleo Mayo (recipe, page 305)

1 tablespoon Dijon-Style Mustard (recipe, page 304)

4 coconut wraps

2 cups baby romaine lettuce

1 recipe Quick Pickles

It is amazing how much flavor the cucumber slices soak up from the vinegar, garlic, dill, vinegar, and pineapple juice in just 15 minutes of standing time. The flavor and crunch of the pickles boost these Cuban-style wraps.

For pork filling, in a large skillet heat oil over medium heat. Add onion and garlic; cook 3 minutes or until onion is softened. Add pork; sprinkle with cumin, oregano, and crushed red pepper. Cook 4 to 5 minutes or until pork is heated through. Stir in orange juice and lime juice; cook 1 minute more. Remove skillet from heat.

In a small bowl stir together Paleo Mayo and Dijon-Style Mustard; spread on wraps. Top with romaine and pork filling and roll up. Serve with Quick Pickles.

Quick Pickles: In a medium bowl combine 1 cucumber, thinly sliced; 3 cloves garlic, smashed; and 1 tablespoon chopped fresh dill. In a small saucepan heat 1 cup white or apple cider vinegar and ½ cup unsweetened pineapple juice to boiling; pour over cucumber mixture. Let stand 15 minutes. Stir in 2 cups ice cubes to quickly cool pickles. When cool, drain pickles in colander; discard any remaining ice.

ROASTED TENDERLOIN >> AND ASPARAGUS WITH MINT- << WATERCRESS PESTO

MAKES **4** SERVINGS

1 1- to 1¼-pound pork tenderloin

2 teaspoons Mediterranean
   Seasoning (recipe, page 296)

6 tablespoons extra virgin olive oil

1 pound fresh asparagus

½ cup slivered onion

½ cup chopped walnuts

1 lemon

¾ cup lightly packed watercress,
   tough stems removed

¼ cup lightly packed fresh mint
   leaves

1 clove garlic, halved

While the tenderloin roasts for 20 to 25 minutes, you make the pesto and prepare the asparagus. It's a tasty, elegant dinner you could serve to company that can be made in 30 minutes or less.

Preheat oven to 425°F. Sprinkle tenderloin all over with Mediterranean Seasoning and drizzle with 1 tablespoon of the olive oil; rub in with your fingers. Place tenderloin on a foil-lined baking sheet. Roast, uncovered, 20 to 25 minutes or until an instant-read thermometer inserted in thickest part of roast registers 145°F.

Meanwhile, snap off and discard woody portions from asparagus. Place asparagus in a 15×10×1-inch baking pan. Add onion; drizzle with 2 tablespoons of the oil; toss to coat. Roast, uncovered, alongside the pork, 10 to 12 minutes or just until asparagus is tender, stirring once halfway through roasting.

For mint-watercress pesto, in a small dry skillet toast the walnuts over medium heat 3 to 4 minutes or until golden, stirring occasionally. Remove ½ teaspoon zest and squeeze 1 tablespoon juice from lemon. In a food processor combine half of the walnuts, the watercress, mint, and garlic. Cover and pulse until finely chopped. Add the remaining 3 tablespoons oil and the lemon zest and juice. Cover and pulse until nearly smooth.

Remove pork and asparagus from the oven. Cover pork with foil; let stand 3 to 5 minutes. Thinly slice the pork. Divide pork and asparagus among four plates. Sprinkle asparagus with the remaining toasted walnuts. Spoon mint-watercress pesto over sliced pork.

JAMAICAN JERK
>> PORK MEDALLIONS <<

MAKES **2** SERVINGS

1 12-ounce pork tenderloin

4 teaspoons Jamaican Jerk
   Seasoning (recipe, page 296)

2 tablespoons coconut oil

1 10-ounce package frozen diced
   sweet potatoes

⅛ teaspoon granulated garlic
   Dash cayenne pepper

This delicious dish featuring Jamaican Jerk-spiced pork and mashed sweet potatoes takes just 20 minutes to get on the table.

Cut pork crosswise into ½-inch slices. Sprinkle pork with 3 teaspoons of the Jamaican Jerk Seasoning.

In a large skillet heat 1 tablespoon of the coconut oil over medium heat. Add pork slices to skillet; cook 6 to 8 minutes until cooked through, turning once.

Meanwhile, in a medium saucepan combine sweet potatoes and enough water to cover. Bring to boiling; reduce heat. Cover and simmer 5 to 7 minutes or until tender. Drain potatoes. Using a potato masher, mash sweet potatoes. Stir in the remaining 1 tablespoon coconut oil, the remaining 1 teaspoon Jamaican Jerk Seasoning, the garlic, and cayenne pepper. Serve with pork.

BALSAMIC-GLAZED PORK
>> TENDERLOIN WITH ROASTED <<
BROCCOLI RAAB AND GRAPES

MAKES **4** SERVINGS

3 tablespoons extra virgin
   olive oil

2 1-pound pork tenderloins

¼ cup balsamic vinegar

2 tablespoons Dijon-Style Mustard
   (recipe, page 304)

1 tablespoon snipped fresh
   rosemary

8 ounces seedless red grapes

1 pound broccoli raab, trimmed

3 tablespoons chopped walnuts
   or sliced almonds, toasted (tip,
   page 63)

Look for young and slender broccoli raab. It will be more tender and sweeter than more mature broccoli raab, which can be bitter.

Preheat oven to 425°F. Brush a baking pan with 1 tablespoon of the oil. Place pork in the prepared pan.

For the glaze, in a small bowl stir together vinegar, Dijon-Style Mustard, and rosemary. Brush pork generously with the glaze. Set aside remaining glaze.

Roast tenderloins 15 minutes; brush with reserved glaze.

Meanwhile, snip grapes into small clusters. Place grape clusters and broccoli raab in a second baking pan. Drizzle the remaining 2 tablespoons oil over grapes and broccoli raab; toss gently to coat. Place in the oven alongside the pork. Roast 10 minutes more or until pork is 145°F, broccoli raab is crisp-tender and beginning to char, and grapes are slightly softened but not mushy.

Let pork stand 5 minutes before slicing. Sprinkle broccoli raab and grapes with nuts; serve with pork.

ROSEMARY PORK
>>   KABOBS WITH MAYO-CHIVE   <<
BROCCOLI SLAW

MAKES 4 SERVINGS

1 to 1¼ pounds pork tenderloin, cut into 1-inch pieces

1 tablespoon extra virgin olive oil

2 teaspoons dried rosemary, crushed

1 teaspoon garlic powder

½ teaspoon black pepper

⅓ cup Paleo Mayo (recipe, page 305)

2 to 3 tablespoons fresh lemon juice

2 tablespoons snipped fresh chives

2 teaspoons Dijon-Style Mustard (recipe, page 304)

1 12-ounce package broccoli slaw mix

Be sure to use metal skewers to make these grilled pork kabobs. Wooden skewers need to be soaked in water for 30 minutes before being used to prevent them from burning.

Drizzle pork with olive oil and sprinkle with rosemary, garlic powder, and pepper; toss to coat evenly. Thread the pork onto 8-inch skewers, leaving a ¼-inch space between pieces.

Grill kabobs, covered, over medium heat about 10 minutes or until pork is cooked through (145°F), turning kabobs once halfway through grilling. (Or cook kabobs on a stove-top grill pan over medium heat.)

Meanwhile, for mayo-chive broccoli slaw, in a medium bowl combine Paleo Mayo, lemon juice, chives, and Dijon-Style Mustard. Add the broccoli slaw mix; stir to combine. Serve with pork kabobs.

>> PORK STIR-FRY <<

MAKES **4** SERVINGS

1½ pounds pork tenderloin

2 teaspoons Smoky Seasoning
(recipe, page 296)

3 tablespoons coconut oil

1 medium onion, halved lengthwise
and sliced

1 medium red or yellow sweet
pepper, cut into bite-size strips

1 8-ounce package fresh shiitake
mushrooms, stems removed
and sliced

1 tablespoon minced fresh ginger

3 cloves garlic, minced

2 cups shredded napa cabbage

¼ cup unsalted chicken stock

¼ cup unsweetened pineapple juice

2 tablespoons sherry vinegar or
white wine vinegar

½ cup unsalted roasted cashews

¼ cup sliced scallions

Cooking the pork in two batches ensures that it caramelizes and takes on a delicious brown crust. If it cooked all at once, it would steam instead of sauté, which would make it soggy and not nearly as appealing.

Cut pork into 2-inch strips; sprinkle with Smoky Seasoning. In a large wok or extra-large skillet heat 1 tablespoon of the coconut oil over medium-high heat. Add half of the pork; cook and stir 4 to 5 minutes or until no longer pink. Remove pork to a bowl. Repeat with another 1 tablespoon oil and the remaining pork. Remove all pork to the bowl; cover to keep warm.

In the same wok add the remaining 1 tablespoon oil. Add onion and sweet pepper; cook and stir 2 minutes. Add mushrooms; cook and stir 3 to 4 minutes or until mushrooms begin to brown. Add ginger and garlic; cook and stir 1 minute more. Add cabbage; cook just until wilted. Remove vegetables from wok.

Add stock, pineapple juice, and vinegar to wok. Bring to boiling; boil to reduce slightly. Return pork and vegetables to wok; heat through, stirring to combine. Stir in cashews and scallions.

PORK TENDERLOIN
>> MEDALLIONS WITH CREAMY <<
MUSTARD-HERB SAUCE

MAKES **4** SERVINGS

¼ cup extra virgin olive oil

2 medium leeks (white and light green parts), cut in half lengthwise and thinly sliced*

1 cup unsalted chicken stock

½ cup dry white wine

2 cloves garlic, minced

½ cup Cashew Cream (recipe, page 304)

2 tablespoons Dijon-Style Mustard (recipe, page 304)

2 tablespoons chopped fresh chives

1 tablespoon chopped fresh dill

2 12-ounce pork tenderloins, each cut into 4 slices

Black pepper

2 tablespoons chopped fresh parsley

Leeks belong to the genus Allium, *along with onion, garlic, shallots, and scallions, and have a delicate onion flavor. Before using them it is essential to clean them well because dirt and grit can collect between the layers (see tip, below). Leek tops should be dark green and firm and bulb ends should have small roots.*

For the sauce, in a large skillet heat 2 tablespoons of the olive oil over medium-high heat. Add leeks; cook 5 minutes or until they begin to turn golden, stirring frequently. Stir in stock, wine, and garlic. Bring to boiling. Cook, uncovered, until reduced to about 1⅔ cups, about 4 minutes. Whisk in Cashew Cream, Dijon-Style Mustard, chives, and dill. Transfer to a bowl; set aside. Wipe the skillet with paper towels.

Firmly press each slice of pork with the palm of your hand to flatten slightly. Sprinkle pork with pepper. Heat the remaining 2 tablespoons oil in skillet over medium-high heat. Add pork; cook about 8 minutes or until done, turning once halfway through cooking.

Add sauce to skillet with pork. Simmer over medium heat about 2 minutes or just until slightly thickened, scraping up any browned bits from bottom of skillet. Season to taste with pepper. Sprinkle with parsley.

*Tip: Wash leeks before using. Place sliced leeks in a bowl of cold water, swirling to remove any sand or grit. Drain in a fine-mesh strainer and pat dry with paper towels or spin dry in a salad spinner.

PORK CHOPS WITH
MANGO CHUTNEY

>>   <<

MAKES **4** SERVINGS

1 **10-ounce package frozen mango chunks**

1 **medium shallot, chopped**

⅓ **cup apple cider**

2 **teaspoons grated fresh ginger**

2½ **teaspoons salt-free garam masala**

¼ **teaspoon crushed red pepper**

¼ **cup unsulfured golden raisins**

1 **tablespoon cider vinegar or sherry vinegar**

4 **boneless pork loin chops, cut ¾ to 1 inch thick**

2 **tablespoons coconut oil**

This dish of pan-fried pork chops accompanied by a chutney spiked with ginger, shallot, garam masala, golden raisins, and crushed red pepper is so delicious and quick to fix, there is no reason to put up with a boring dinner, no matter how busy your evening is.

For mango chutney, in a medium saucepan combine mango, shallot, apple cider, ginger, ½ teaspoon of the garam masala, and the crushed red pepper. Bring to boiling; reduce heat. Simmer, uncovered, 5 minutes or until mango has softened and liquid has reduced slightly. Remove from heat; stir in raisins and vinegar. Let stand at room temperature until serving.

Meanwhile, sprinkle both sides of pork chops with the remaining 2 teaspoons garam masala. In a large skillet heat coconut oil over medium heat. Add chops to skillet; cook 8 to 10 minutes or until slightly pink in centers (145°F), turning once halfway through cooking.

Serve pork chops with mango chutney.

PORK CHOPS WITH
>> QUICK PEAR CHUTNEY <<

MAKES **4** SERVINGS

1   shallot, diced
3   tablespoons cider vinegar
2   tablespoons fresh orange juice
1   tablespoon coconut oil
1   1-inch piece peeled fresh ginger, thinly sliced
1   cinnamon stick
1   teaspoon Madras curry powder
¼   teaspoon crushed red pepper
3   ripe pears, peeled, cored, and coarsely chopped
¼   cup unsulfured, unsweetened dried cranberries or tart cherries
8   thin bone-in pork chops (about 4 ounces each)
    Black pepper
2   tablespoons extra virgin olive oil
2   tablespoons chopped fresh cilantro

The microwave can be used for so much more than reheating leftovers. It is a handy tool that is underused in preparing fresh, healthful meals. Here, the chutney cooks down to a thick, juicy consistency in the microwave while the chops are pan-fried. Right before serving, the chutney is added to the skillet to pick up drippings from the meat.

For chutney, in a microwave-safe bowl combine shallot, vinegar, orange juice, coconut oil, ginger, cinnamon stick, curry powder, and crushed red pepper. Cover with plastic wrap (do not vent). Microwave 1 minute. Stir in pears and cranberries. Replace plastic wrap, microwave 10 minutes more. Poke holes in plastic wrap to release steam.

Pat pork chops dry with paper towels and sprinkle with black pepper. In a large skillet heat 1 tablespoon of the olive oil over medium-high heat. Add four of the chops to the hot oil; cook about 3 minutes or until golden on one side. Flip chops and cook 1 minute or until cooked through. Remove chops to a plate and tent with foil to keep warm. Repeat with the remaining oil and chops; remove all chops to plate.

Add chutney to drippings in skillet. Cook and stir over low heat, scraping up any crusty brown bits that cling to bottom of skillet. Simmer until slightly thickened. Discard cinnamon stick. Serve warm chutney with chops. Sprinkle with cilantro.

DIJON PORK CHOPS
>> WITH GARLIC GREENS <<

MAKES **4** SERVINGS

3 tablespoons Dijon-Style Mustard
(recipe, page 304)

2 tablespoons apple cider

3 tablespoons extra virgin olive oil

4 bone-in pork chops, cut
¾ to 1 inch thick

1 tablespoon Mediterranean
Seasoning (recipe, page 296)

2 medium onions, halved
lengthwise and thinly sliced

6 cloves garlic, thinly sliced

2 bunches Swiss chard, trimmed
and coarsely chopped

Dijon-Style Mustard (recipe, page 304) doesn't have any added salt—and it doesn't need it. The head-clearing condiment is made only with brown mustard seeds, cider vinegar, white wine, turmeric, and a little water. It is pretty powerful when it is first made, but it mellows over time. It's a good condiment to have on hand. Just a little bit infuses food with amazing flavor.

Preheat broiler. For glaze, in a small bowl combine Dijon-Style Mustard, apple cider, and 1 tablespoon of the olive oil.

Sprinkle both sides of pork chops with Mediterranean Seasoning. Place pork chops on the unheated rack of a broiler pan. Broil 3 to 4 inches from heat 8 to 10 minutes or until slightly pink in centers (145°F), brushing both sides with glaze and turning once halfway through broiling. (Discard remaining glaze.)

Meanwhile, in an extra-large skillet heat the remaining 2 tablespoons olive oil over medium heat. Add onions; cook and stir 5 to 6 minutes or until softened and beginning to brown. Add garlic; cook and stir 30 seconds or until fragrant. Add Swiss chard; cook and stir 2 to 3 minutes or just until wilted. Serve with pork chops.

SMASHED GARLIC-SAGE CHOPS
WITH ZUCCHINI NOODLES

>> <<

MAKES 4 SERVINGS

4 bone-in pork rib chops, cut
   1½ inches thick

2 teaspoons black pepper

2 tablespoons extra virgin olive oil

1 8-ounce package sliced fresh
   mushrooms

4 cloves garlic, smashed

16 fresh sage leaves

5 large zucchini, cut into noodles*

1 recipe Chimichurri Sauce
   (recipe, page 305)

Sage and pork are a natural pairing. There is something about the earthy, pungent flavor of sage that complements the mildly sweet flavor of pork. In this dish, smashed cloves of garlic are briefly cooked, so they still pack a lot of punch. (Pictured on pages 88-89.)

Sprinkle both sides of chops with pepper. In an extra-large skillet heat olive oil over medium-high heat. Add chops to skillet; cook 8 to 12 minutes or until slightly pink in centers (145°F), turning twice. Remove chops to serving platter; cover to keep warm.

Add mushrooms to the hot skillet; cook over medium-high heat 3 minutes. Add smashed garlic and sage leaves; cook 1 minute. Spoon over chops.

Add zucchini to skillet; cook 2 minutes. Toss zucchini with Chimichurri Sauce. Serve zucchini with chops.

*Tip:** Trim ends off zucchini. Use a vegetable spiralizer, julienne cutter, or mandoline to cut zucchini into long, thin noodles.

Spicy Pork Chops with Grilled
Zucchini and Watermelon-
Grapefruit Salsa, recipe, page 114

SPICY PORK CHOPS WITH GRILLED ZUCCHINI AND WATERMELON-GRAPEFRUIT SALSA

>>   <<

MAKES **4** SERVINGS

1 tablespoon black pepper

2 teaspoons smoked paprika

1½ teaspoons onion powder

1 teaspoon garlic powder

1 teaspoon ground cumin

1 teaspoon ground ancho chile pepper

4 bone-in pork chops, cut 1½ inches thick

2 ruby red, pink, or white grapefruit, peeled and sectioned*

2 cups seedless watermelon chunks

½ cup finely chopped red onion

¼ cup chopped fresh cilantro or basil

1 jalapeño chile, seeded if desired and finely chopped (tip, page 37)

2 tablespoons fresh lime juice

2 tablespoons extra virgin olive oil

½ teaspoon black pepper

2 zucchini, sliced ¼ inch thick

2 teaspoons extra virgin olive oil

If you need to grill on a stove-top grill pan, this recipe will take a little bit longer than 30 minutes because you will need to grill the chops and zucchini separately, because everything won't fit on the grill pan at once.

For spice rub, in a small bowl stir together the 1 tablespoon black pepper, the paprika, onion powder, garlic powder, cumin, and ground ancho chile pepper. Sprinkle on both sides of chops. Set chops aside while making the salsa.

For watermelon-grapefruit salsa, in a medium bowl combine grapefruit, watermelon, onion, cilantro, jalapeño, lime juice, the 2 tablespoons olive oil, and the ½ teaspoon black pepper. Stir gently.

Grill chops, covered, over medium heat 12 minutes or until slightly pink in centers (145°F), turning once halfway through grilling. Brush zucchini slices with the 2 teaspoons olive oil. Grill zucchini alongside chops 6 minutes or until crisp-tender and grill marks appear. (Or grill chops and zucchini on a stove-top grill pan over medium heat.)

Serve chops and zucchini with watermelon-grapefruit salsa.

*Tip: To section citrus fruit, cut a thin slice off the top and bottom of the fruit. Slice off the peel from top to bottom, following the curve of fruit. Holding the fruit over a bowl, use a sharp knife to cut between the membranes and each segment, allowing the segments to fall into the bowl.

MUSHROOM PÂTÉ-
>> STUFFED PORK CHOPS <<

MAKES 4 SERVINGS

8 wooden toothpicks

½ cup slivered almonds

½ cup purchased sliced button or
    cremini mushrooms

½ of a medium shallot, cut up

2 tablespoons coconut oil

2 teaspoons snipped fresh sage or
    ½ teaspoon dried sage, crushed

4 boneless pork chops, cut 1 inch
    thick

½ teaspoon garlic powder

½ teaspoon black pepper

¼ teaspoon onion powder

¾ cup unsalted chicken stock

4 cups fresh baby spinach

½ cup halved cherry or grape
    tomatoes

⅓ cup Roasted Garlic Vinaigrette
    (recipe, page 300)

The stuffed chops are browned in the skillet to create a beautiful brown exterior and then finished in the oven. While they roast, toss together a simple salad of baby spinach, cherry tomatoes, slivered toasted almonds, and a spicy vinaigrette.

Soak toothpicks in enough water to cover. Preheat oven to 425°F. In an extra-large oven-going skillet heat slivered almonds over medium heat 2 to 3 minutes or until lightly toasted, stirring occasionally. Remove almonds from skillet; set aside. In a food processor combine mushrooms and shallot; cover and pulse until finely chopped. Add mushroom mixture to the same skillet along with 1 tablespoon of the oil. Cook 3 to 4 minutes or until tender and lightly browned, stirring occasionally.

Wipe the food processor dry. Add half of the toasted almonds to the processor. Cover and process until coarsely ground. Use the remaining almonds in the spinach salad. In a small bowl combine cooked mushroom mixture, ground almonds, and sage.

Make a pocket in each pork chop by cutting horizontally from the outside edge almost to the bone. Spoon mushroom pâté into pockets. Secure openings with the wooden toothpicks. Sprinkle chops with garlic powder, pepper, and onion powder.

In the same extra-large skillet heat the remaining 1 tablespoon oil over medium-high heat. Add chops to skillet. Cook 4 to 6 minutes or until browned, turning once to brown both sides. Carefully add stock. Bring to boiling.

Place skillet with chops in the oven. Roast, uncovered, 10 to 12 minutes or until 145°F. Let chops rest 3 minutes.

Meanwhile, for salad, in a large bowl combine spinach, remaining toasted almonds, tomatoes, and vinaigrette. Toss to combine. Serve with chops.

GRILLED PORK CHOPS
>> WITH CABBAGE <<

4 boneless pork chops, cut ½ inch
    thick

¾ cup Mango-Lime Salad Dressing
    (recipe, page 300)

1 small head green cabbage

2 to 3 tablespoons water

2 tablespoons coconut oil, melted

2 teaspoons sesame seeds, toasted
    (tip, page 69)

1 tablespoon chopped fresh
    cilantro

The humble cabbage is a far more versatile vegetable than you might think. It's terrific roasted in wedges or thick slices, brushed with olive oil, and seasoned with black pepper and fennel seeds. It's also wonderful grilled. Here, it gets a head start in the microwave and is finished up on the grill for a smoky flavor.

Place pork chops in a large resealable plastic bag. Add ½ cup of the Mango-Lime Salad Dressing. Seal bag; turn to coat chops. Let stand at room temperature 15 minutes, turning bag occasionally.

Meanwhile, cut cabbage into quarters, keeping the core intact. Place cabbage in a microwave-safe 2-quart square baking dish; add the water. Cover loosely with plastic wrap or waxed paper. Microwave 6 to 8 minutes or until nearly tender, turning and rearranging cabbage twice. Drain; brush cabbage with melted coconut oil.

Remove chops from the marinade; discard marinade. Grill chops over medium heat 6 to 8 minutes or until slightly pink in centers (145°F), turning once halfway through grilling. Grill cabbage alongside chops 6 to 8 minutes or until tender and lightly charred, turning occasionally. (Or cook chops and cabbage on a stove-top grill pan over medium heat.)

Remove chops from grill; cover and let stand 3 minutes. Meanwhile, place a cabbage quarter on each of four serving plates; drizzle with the remaining ¼ cup Mango-Lime Salad Dressing and sprinkle with sesame seeds. Add a chop to each plate; sprinkle with cilantro.

PAN-SEARED PORK CUTLETS WITH DRIED TOMATO-ZUCCHINI HASH

MAKES **4** SERVINGS

- 6 tablespoons extra virgin olive oil or coconut oil
- 1 medium sweet onion, diced
- 2 medium zucchini, diced
- 1 teaspoon black pepper
- ⅓ cup slivered dried tomatoes (not oil-packed)
- 2 tablespoons dry white wine or unsalted beef stock
- 1 cup finely chopped almonds
- 1 tablespoon snipped fresh rosemary
- 4 boneless pork chops, cut ½ inch thick

Even small amounts dried tomatoes add an appealingly chewy texture and intense tomato flavor to dishes. Be sure to use dried tomatoes that don't have any added ingredients, like sulfur dioxide and salt.

For tomato-zucchini hash, in a large skillet heat 2 tablespoons of the oil over medium-high heat. Cook onion in the hot oil 2 minutes, stirring frequently. Add zucchini; sprinkle with ½ teaspoon of the pepper. Cook 5 minutes or until vegetables are tender and browned, stirring occasionally. Stir in tomatoes and wine. Cook 1 minute; remove skillet from heat. Cover hash to keep warm.

Meanwhile, using the flat side of a meat mallet, flatten pork between two pieces of plastic wrap to ¼ inch thick. In a shallow bowl combine almonds, rosemary, and the remaining ½ teaspoon pepper. Dip both sides of pork chops in almond mixture.

In an extra-large skillet heat the remaining 4 tablespoons oil over medium-high heat. Cook pork in hot oil 2 to 3 minutes or until slightly pink in centers (145°F), turning once halfway through cooking. Serve pork with hash.

>> BAYOU COUNTRY PORK STEW <<

MAKES 4 SERVINGS

1 pound boneless pork country-
   style ribs, cut into ½-inch pieces

2 tablespoons coconut oil

4 cups unsalted chicken stock

1 cup frozen mirepoix blend
   vegetables (chopped onion,
   celery, and carrots)

2 teaspoons Cajun Seasoning
   (recipe, page 296)

1 bay leaf

1 medium summer squash, cut into
   1-inch pieces, or 8 pattypan
   squash, trimmed and quartered

3 cups coarsely chopped, trimmed
   collard greens

1 14.5-ounce can no-salt-added
   stewed tomatoes

1 cup frozen cut okra

½ cup chopped fresh parsley

A frozen mirepoix blend gives you a leg up on the knife work for this Southern-style stew. It is readily available, but if you can't find it, combine ⅓ cup each chopped onion, celery, and carrots. It will take a little bit longer—but not much—to prepare the recipe.

In a 4- to 6-quart Dutch oven cook pork in hot coconut oil over medium-high heat 3 to 5 minutes or until browned, stirring occasionally. Remove pork from Dutch oven.

Add stock, mirepoix vegetables, Cajun Seasoning, and bay leaf to Dutch oven. Bring to boiling; reduce heat. Cover and simmer 5 minutes. Add squash; cover and simmer 5 minutes. Add collard greens; cover and simmer 5 minutes more. Using kitchen scissors, cut up tomatoes in the can. Add undrained tomatoes, cooked pork, and okra to the stew. Return to boiling; cover and cook 5 minutes or until meat and vegetables are tender.

Discard bay leaf. Stir ¼ cup of the parsley into the stew. Ladle stew into serving bowls; sprinkle with the remaining parsley.

>> BARBECUED PORK SHEPHERD'S PIE <<

MAKES **4** SERVINGS

1 pound ground pork

½ cup thinly sliced celery

1 cup frozen chopped onion and
  green sweet pepper blend

1 10-ounce package frozen pureed
  butternut squash

1 teaspoon Smoky Seasoning
  (recipe, page 296)

2 cups packaged fresh baby
  spinach

¾ cup BBQ Sauce (recipe,
  page 305)

½ teaspoon ground cumin
  Smoky Seasoning (recipe,
  page 296)
  Chopped fresh parsley

Drain the cooked pureed squash well before stirring in the seasoning and spreading it over the pie so that you have minimal liquid left in the dish after baking.

Preheat oven to 425°F. In a large skillet cook pork, celery, and onion and sweet pepper blend over medium heat until meat is browned and vegetables are tender.

Meanwhile, place squash in a microwave-safe medium bowl; cover loosely with plastic wrap. Microwave on 70% power (medium-high) 6 minutes or until heated through, stirring twice. Place squash in a fine-mesh sieve and allow excess liquid to drain. Return squash to the bowl; stir in the 1 teaspoon Smoky Seasoning.

Drain fat from the pork mixture. Add spinach, BBQ Sauce, and cumin to skillet. Cook 1 to 2 minutes or until heated through. Spoon pork mixture into a 1½-quart casserole or baking dish. Spread hot squash over pork mixture.

Bake, uncovered, 10 minutes or until heated through and squash is lightly browned. Sprinkle with additional Smoky Seasoning and the parsley.

ASIAN GROUND PORK AND LETTUCE WRAPS

>> <<

MAKES **4** SERVINGS

1 tablespoon sesame seeds

1 tablespoon coconut oil

½ cup minced shallots

2 tablespoons minced fresh ginger

2 cloves garlic, minced

2 teaspoons salt-free Chinese five-spice powder

1 pound ground pork

1 cup finely chopped red sweet pepper

½ cup finely chopped no-salt-added water chestnuts

6 scallions, sliced

1 head Bibb lettuce, leaves separated

Water chestnuts give the ginger- and garlic-infused filling for these lettuce wraps lots of crunch. Be sure to use only canned water chestnuts that have no added salt or other non-Paleo ingredients.

In a dry large skillet toast the sesame seeds over medium heat about 3 minutes or until golden brown and fragrant, stirring often. Remove sesame seeds to a plate; let cool.

In the same skillet heat the coconut oil over medium-high heat. Add shallots, ginger, and garlic. Cook and stir 4 minutes or until onions are translucent. Stir in the five-spice powder; cook about 30 seconds or until very fragrant.

Add pork and sweet pepper to skillet; cook until meat begins to brown. Stir in water chestnuts. Cook 8 minutes or until the pork is no longer pink. Stir in scallions.

Divide pork filling among lettuce leaves. Sprinkle with toasted sesame seeds.

CAJUN PORK AND COLLARD GREEN HASH

>>   <<

MAKES 4 SERVINGS

1 tablespoon extra virgin olive oil

1 pound ground pork

2 to 3 tablespoons Cajun Seasoning (recipe, page 296)

2 medium red and/or green sweet peppers, seeded and chopped

1½ cups sliced celery

½ cup chopped onion

1 jalapeño chile, seeded and coarsely chopped (tip, page 37)

1 bunch collard greens, trimmed and coarsely chopped

1 cup grape tomatoes, halved

This spicy dish includes what is referred to as the "holy trinity" in Cajun cooking— sweet peppers, celery, and onion. Use the larger amount of Cajun Seasoning if you like your food spicy.

In a large skillet heat oil over medium heat. Add pork and Cajun Seasoning; cook until pork is browned. Add sweet peppers, celery, onion, and jalapeño; cook 8 minutes or just until vegetables are tender.

Stir collard greens into skillet; cook 4 minutes or just until wilted. Stir in tomatoes and heat through.

KNIFE-AND-FORK PORK BURGERS
>> WITH CHARRED SCALLION MAYO <<

MAKES 4 BURGERS

1   cucumber, thinly sliced

1   small red onion, thinly sliced

2   tablespoons snipped fresh dill

1   cup all-natural apple cider

1   cup apple cider vinegar

2   cups ice cubes

1½ pounds ground pork

2   teaspoons Lemon-Herb
    Seasoning (recipe, page 296)

2   cloves garlic, minced

4   scallions, trimmed

1   teaspoon extra virgin olive oil

½   teaspoon black pepper

½   cup Paleo Mayo (recipe,
    page 305)

¼   teaspoon onion powder

2   large heirloom tomatoes, cored
    and cut crosswise into ½-inch
    slices

4   cups arugula or baby spinach

You won't miss the bun on these hefty pork burgers flavored with Lemon-Herb Seasoning and garlic. The rich scallion mayo and crisp pickled cucumber-onion salad are terrific complementary companions.

For the quick pickled cucumber-onion salad, in a medium bowl combine cucumber, onion, and dill. In a small saucepan combine cider and vinegar. Bring to boiling; pour over cucumber and onion. Let stand 15 minutes. Stir in ice cubes. Let stand while preparing burgers.

In a large bowl combine ground pork, Lemon-Herb Seasoning, and garlic. Form into four patties. Grill burgers, uncovered, over medium heat about 10 minutes or until done (160°F), turning once halfway through grilling. (Or cook burgers on a stove-top grill pan over medium heat.)

Meanwhile, for charred scallion mayo, toss scallions with the olive oil and pepper. Grill scallions about 3 minutes or until lightly charred, turning once. Thinly slice the scallions. In a small bowl stir together the scallions, Paleo Mayo, and onion powder.

To assemble, place 1 tomato slice on each of four plates. Top each with 1 cup arugula, a burger, some of the mayo, and another tomato slice.

Drain cucumber-onion salad (discard any remaining ice) and serve with burgers.

GRILLED BBQ PORK PATTIES
WITH PINEAPPLE

>>   <<

MAKES 4 SERVINGS

1 peeled and cored fresh pineapple

1½ pounds ground pork

¾ cup BBQ Sauce (recipe, page 305)

½ cup chopped scallions

½ cup chopped fresh cilantro

1 tablespoon extra virgin olive oil

4 cups mixed baby greens

The Paleo BBQ Sauce (recipe, page 305) does double duty here. It's mixed in with the meat for the patties and is then drizzled over the top of the cooked patties and salad greens as well. The smoky flavor of the sauce is wonderful with rings of grilled pineapple.

Slice pineapple crosswise into eight slices; set aside.

In a large bowl combine pork, ¼ cup of the BBQ Sauce, ¼ cup of the scallions, and ¼ cup of the cilantro. Shape into four ¾-inch-thick patties. Brush patties lightly with the olive oil.

Grill patties, uncovered, over medium heat 10 to 12 minutes or until done (160°F), turning once halfway through grilling. Grill pineapple alongside patties 6 to 8 minutes or until grill marks appear, turning once halfway through grilling. (Or cook pork patties and pineapple slices on a stove-top grill pan over medium heat.)

Divide greens among four serving plates. Place pork patties on greens; top with the remaining BBQ Sauce, scallions, and cilantro. Serve with grilled pineapple.

MIDDLE EASTERN MEATBALLS
>> WITH GRILLED CAULIFLOWER <<

½ cup almond meal

6 cloves garlic, minced

2 teaspoons ground coriander

1 teaspoon ground cumin

½ teaspoon ground allspice

½ teaspoon ground cardamom

½ teaspoon cayenne pepper

1 egg, lightly beaten

1½ pounds ground pork

2 small heads cauliflower

4 tablespoons extra virgin olive oil

½ teaspoon black pepper

1 clove garlic, halved

½ cup Cashew Cream (recipe, page 304)

¼ cup chopped fresh mint

¼ cup chopped fresh parsley

¼ cup slivered almonds, toasted (tip, page 63)

Although pork is not eaten much in Middle Eastern cuisine, spices from that part of the world—coriander, cumin, allspice, cardamom, and cayenne—are particularly good in these crusty pork meatballs. Planks of grilled cauliflower, a fresh mint-parsley garnish, and a cooling sauce made with Cashew Cream (recipe, page 304) round out the dish.

Preheat oven to 400°F. For the spice blend, in a small bowl combine coriander, cumin, allspice, cardamom, and cayenne pepper. In a large bowl combine egg, almond meal, minced garlic, and 3¼ teaspoons of the spice blend. Add ground pork, mix well. Shape meat into thirty-two 1½-inch meatballs and place on a baking pan. Bake 15 to 20 minutes or until cooked through (160°F).

Trim outer leaves from the cauliflower heads, keeping cores intact. Place cauliflower heads, stem sides down, on a cutting board. Cut two 1-inch-thick slices from the center of each of the heads for a total of four planks. (Save the remaining cauliflower for another use.) Brush cauliflower slices with 2 tablespoons of the olive oil. Sprinkle with black pepper.

Grill cauliflower, uncovered, over medium heat 8 to 10 minutes or until crisp-tender and grill marks appear, turning once halfway through grilling. (Or cook cauliflower on a stove-top grill pan over medium heat.) Remove cauliflower from grill; rub both sides of cauliflower with the cut sides of garlic halves.

In a small bowl combine Cashew Cream and remaining 1 teaspoon spice blend. In another bowl combine mint, parsley, almonds, and remaining 2 tablespoons oil. Place a cauliflower slice and eight meatballs on each of four serving plates. Spoon herb mixture over cauliflower slices and meatballs. Drizzle with spiced Cashew Cream.

PORK MINI MEAT LOAVES
>> WITH APPLE-PARSNIP HASH <<

1 egg, lightly beaten

½ cup finely chopped unsulfured
   dried apricots

⅓ cup almond meal

2 teaspoons Mediterranean
   Seasoning (recipe, page 296)

½ teaspoon black pepper

1 pound ground pork

3 tablespoons Dijon-Style Mustard
   (recipe, page 304)

2 red-skin cooking apples, chopped

1 medium leek, thinly sliced

½ cup thinly sliced celery

1 large parsnip, peeled and cut into
   ½-inch pieces

1 tablespoon coconut oil

4 cups coarsely chopped and
   trimmed mustard greens

¼ cup unsweetened apple juice

¼ cup dry white wine

Certain varieties of apples are better for cooking than others that are best eaten fresh out of hand. Cooking apples tend to hold their shape better than other types of apples when exposed to heat. Good apple choices for this dish include Jonagold, Empire, Cortland, and Braeburn.

Preheat oven to 425°F. Line a 15×10×1-inch baking pan with parchment paper.

In a large bowl combine egg, apricots, almond meal, Mediterranean Seasoning, and pepper. Add pork; mix well. Shape meat mixture into four 5×2-inch oval loaves. Place in the prepared baking pan. Spoon Dijon-Style Mustard over meat loaves. Bake 15 minutes or until cooked through (160°F).

Meanwhile, for hash, in a large skillet cook apples, leek, celery, and parsnip in hot coconut oil over medium heat 4 minutes, stirring occasionally. Add mustard greens, apple juice, and wine; cook 2 minutes. Serve with meat loaves.

>> SPICY PORK WITH HERBS <<

MAKES 4 SERVINGS

1 pound ground pork

3 tablespoons coconut oil

2 teaspoons smoked paprika

1 teaspoon crushed red pepper

1 teaspoon cumin seeds

2 cloves garlic, minced

1 medium head cauliflower, broken into florets

2 tablespoons coarsely chopped almonds, toasted (tip, page 63)

2 teaspoons lemon zest

¼ cup snipped fresh parsley

¼ cup snipped fresh mint

Crushed red pepper (optional)

Lemon wedges

This unusual method of cooking pork calls for 1 pound of meat to be divided into two large patties and then cooked over medium-high heat until browned and very crisp. The patties are then broken up into pieces; seasoned with smoked paprika, crushed red pepper, cumin, and garlic; and cooked until done. The result is fabulously crispy chunks of pork served over cauliflower rice studded with toasted almonds and lemon zest.

Form pork into two ¼-inch-thick patties. In an extra-large skillet heat 1 tablespoon of the coconut oil over medium-high heat. Place patties in skillet; cook 3 minutes or until bottoms are browned and very crisp. Carefully turn patties and cook 3 minutes more or until second sides are browned and crisp. Reduce heat to medium. Break patties into small pieces; add smoked paprika, crushed red pepper, cumin, and garlic. Cook 2 to 3 minutes or until spices are fragrant and meat is cooked through.

Meanwhile, in a food processor pulse cauliflower (in batches if necessary) until the pieces are the size of rice. In a large skillet cook cauliflower rice in the remaining coconut oil over medium heat 5 minutes or until tender and just beginning to brown, stirring occasionally. Stir in almonds and lemon zest.

Serve pork over cauliflower rice; sprinkle with parsley, mint, and, if desired, additional crushed red pepper. Pass lemon wedges.

3 WAYS WITH PRECOOKED BEETS

This once-shunned root vegetable has become a culinary darling the last few years, and for good reason. Not only is its sweet, earthy flavor and vibrant color highly appealing, but it is a nutritional powerhouse as well. Beets are especially high in folate—a B vitamin that supports brain and cardiovascular system health—and manganese, which contributes to bone health. However, being a dense vegetable, beets do take some time to roast or steam and would not be ready to eat in 30 minutes or less unless they were precooked. Now more and more supermarkets are carrying packages of refrigerated cooked baby beets that do not contain any ingredients other than beets. The recipes on the following pages—Pork Paillards with Beet-Pear-Marcona Almond Salad (page 39), Dredged Chops with Beet-Apple Salad (page 138), and Moroccan Lamb Burgers with Beet Salsa (page 139)—all take advantage of this perfectly Paleo product.

PORK PAILLARDS
>> WITH BEET-PEAR-MARCONA <<
ALMOND SALAD

MAKES **4** SERVINGS

- 4 boneless pork chops, cut
    ½ inch thick
- Black pepper
- 3 tablespoons extra virgin olive oi
- 2 Anjou pears
- 2 8-ounce packages refrigerated
    cooked baby beets
- ¼ cup Roasted Garlic Vinaigrette
    (recipe, page 300)
- 4 cups baby arugula
- ⅓ cup chopped Marcona almonds
- ¼ cup snipped chives

Marcona almonds are a type of Spanish almond that has a plumper, more rounded shape than regular almonds. Their flavor is rich and mild, with a buttery texture similar to a macadamia nut. They are most often sold at markets fried in olive oil and salted to be eaten as a snack. There are raw, unsalted Marcona almonds available, however. If you like, toast them lightly in a skillet before using.

Using a meat mallet, lightly flatten chops between two pieces of plastic wrap to ¼ inch thick. Sprinkle chops with black pepper. In an extra-large skillet cook chops in hot oil over medium-high heat 6 minutes or until golden brown on each side, turning once.

Halve and core pears; cut into matchstick-size pieces. Cut beets into matchstick-size pieces. In a medium bowl toss pears and beets with Roasted Garlic Vinaigrette.

Place a pork paillard on each of four serving plates. Divide arugula among plates. Top arugula with beets and pears; sprinkle with almonds and chives.

(2)

DREDGED CHOPS WITH
>> BEET-APPLE SALAD <<

MAKES 4 SERVINGS

½ cup coconut flour

½ cup almond flour

2 tablespoons Lemon-Herb or
   Mediterranean Seasoning
   (recipes, page 296)

1 egg, lightly beaten

2 tablespoons water

4 4-to-5-ounce boneless pork
   rib chops

2 tablespoons extra virgin olive oil

1 8-ounce package refrigerated
   cooked baby beets, cut into
   matchstick-size pieces

2 Pink Lady or Fuji apples, cored,
   seeded, and thinly sliced

¼ cup finely chopped sweet onion

¼ cup chopped walnuts, toasted
   (tip, page 63)

½ cup chopped fresh parsley

½ cup Classic French Vinaigrette
   (recipe, page 300)

The coating for these pan-fried chops—made from a blend of almond flour and coconut flour—creates an absolutely delicious, surprisingly crisp crust on the pan-fried chops. You won't miss wheat flour-based breading a bit.

In a shallow dish combine coconut and almond flours and Lemon-Herb or Mediterranean Seasoning. In another shallow dish whisk together egg and the water. Lightly flatten chops with fingertips to ¼-inch thickness. Dip chops in egg mixture, then dredge chops in the flour mixture.

In a large heavy skillet heat oil over medium heat. Add chops; cook 8 to 10 minutes or until done (145°F), turning once halfway through cooking.

Meanwhile, for salad, in a medium bowl combine beets, apples, onion, walnuts, and parsley. Drizzle with Classic French Vinaigrette. Serve with chops.

MOROCCAN LAMB BURGERS
WITH BEET SALSA

>>   <<

MAKES 4 SERVINGS

2 tablespoons extra virgin olive oil

2 tablespoons fresh lemon juice

2 8-ounce packages refrigerated
   cooked baby beets, chopped

2 navel oranges, peeled, sectioned,
   and chopped

½ cup chopped red onion

2 tablespoons snipped fresh
   cilantro

¼ cup minced shallot

2 cloves garlic, minced

2 tablespoons snipped fresh basil

2 tablespoons snipped fresh mint

1 tablespoon ras el hanout

1½ pounds ground lamb

These lamb burgers are flavored with a North African spice blend called ras el hanout. The phrase translates from Arabic to English as "head of the shop," a reference to a blend that is the best a spice shop has to offer. It is most often a mixture of at least a dozen spices. Common ingredients include cardamom, cumin, clove, cinnamon, nutmeg, mace, allspice, dried ginger and chiles, coriander, peppercorn, paprika, fenugreek, and dried turmeric.

For beet salsa, in a medium bowl whisk together olive oil and lemon juice. Add beets, oranges, onion, and cilantro; toss to coat.

In a large bowl combine shallot, garlic, basil, mint, and ras el hanout. Add lamb; mix well. Shape into four ½-inch thick patties.

Grill burgers, uncovered, over medium heat 10 to 12 minutes or until done (160°F), turning once halfway through grilling. (Or cook burgers on a stove-top grill pan over medium heat.) Serve patties topped with salsa.

PESTO LAMB CHOPS
>> WITH FENNEL SALAD <<

MAKES **4** SERVINGS

8 lamb rib chops, cut ½ to ¾ inch thick

½ cup Basil Pesto (recipe, page 301)

2 medium fennel bulbs, trimmed, cored, and thinly shaved*

½ cup thinly sliced red onion

½ cup chopped fresh parsley

¼ cup Roasted Garlic Vinaigrette (recipe, page 300)

With the pantry items—Basil Pesto and Roasted Garlic Vinaigrette—made and ready to go, this elegant recipe goes together in less than 20 minutes.

Brush lamb chops with ¼ cup of the Basil Pesto. Grill chops, covered, over medium heat 6 to 8 minutes for medium rare (145°F) or 10 to 12 minutes for medium (150°F), turning once halfway through grilling. (Or grill lamb chops on a stove-top grill pan over medium heat.)

Meanwhile, for fennel salad, in a medium bowl combine fennel, onion, and parsley. Drizzle with Roasted Garlic Vinaigrette; toss to coat.

Serve lamb chops with the remaining ¼ cup Basil Pesto and the fennel salad.

*Tip: Use a mandoline to shave fennel into very thin slices.

LAMB RIB CHOPS WITH
>> GRAPE TOMATOES OVER <<
SPAGHETTI SQUASH

MAKES **4** SERVINGS

1   2-pound spaghetti squash, halved
    and seeded

8   lamb rib chops, cut 1 inch thick

1½ teaspoons Lemon-Herb
    Seasoning (recipe, page 296)

3   teaspoons extra virgin olive oil

2   cups red and/or yellow cherry
    tomatoes

1   clove garlic, minced
    Snipped fresh thyme (optional)

While the spaghetti squash cooks in the microwave, the lamb chops are seasoned and seared in the skillet. When the lamb chops are done and kept warm, the tomatoes are wilted with garlic in the same skillet—and dinner is done!

Place squash halves, cut sides down, in a microwave-safe baking dish. Cover with vented plastic wrap. Microwave 12 to 15 minutes or until tender. Let cool while preparing chops.

Pat lamb chops dry; rub chops with 1 teaspoon of the Lemon-Herb Seasoning. In a large skillet heat 2 teaspoons of the oil over medium-high heat. Add lamb chops to skillet; cook 9 minutes for medium (160° F), turning once halfway through cooking. Remove chops to a plate; cover to keep warm.

In the same skillet cook tomatoes and garlic in drippings 2 minutes or until tomatoes are heated through and slightly soft, stirring frequently. Remove skillet from heat.

Using a fork, remove the squash pulp from the shell. In a small bowl combine the remaining 1 teaspoon oil and the remaining ½ teaspoon Lemon-Herb Seasoning. Pour over spaghetti squash and toss to coat.

Serve chops and tomatoes over spaghetti squash. If desired, sprinkle with fresh thyme.

Lamb Kefte with
Pomegranate-Orange
Glaze and Sparkling Mint
Salad, *recipe, page 146*

LAMB KEFTE WITH
>> POMEGRANATE-ORANGE GLAZE <<
AND SPARKLING MINT SALAD

MAKES 4 SERVINGS

1   cup fresh orange juice

½   cup pomegranate juice

2   tablespoons chopped fresh mint

1   cup finely chopped onion

¼   cup chopped fresh cilantro

¼   cup chopped fresh mint

2   tablespoons ras el hanout

1   tablespoon lemon zest

2   garlic cloves, minced

1½ pounds ground lamb

2   eggs, lightly beaten

1   recipe Sparkling Mint Salad

Kefte (sometimes spelled kofta) is best known in the Arab world as street food. It usually consists of ground beef, lamb, or chicken that is highly seasoned, then shaped into meatballs, patties, or formed around skewers and grilled.

For pomegranate-orange glaze, bring orange juice and pomegranate juice to boiling; reduce heat. Simmer, uncovered, 20 minutes or until thick and syrupy, and reduced by half. Remove from heat; let cool. Stir the 2 tablespoons mint into cooled glaze.

For the kefte, in a food processor combine onion, cilantro, the ¼ cup mint, the ras el hanut, lemon zest, and garlic; pulse until finely chopped. Add lamb and eggs; pulse just until combined. Form the meat mixture into 3×½-inch ovals or 2×½-inch patties.

Grill keftes, uncovered, over medium heat 4 minutes for medium rare (145°F), turning once. (Or cook keftes on a stove-top grill pan over medium heat.) Immediately drizzle some of the glaze over keftes. Serve with Sparkling Mint Salad and the remaining glaze for dipping.

Sparkling Mint Salad: Cut enough jicama into matchstick-size pieces to make 1 cup. Cut 1 sweet-tart apple (such as Pink Lady) into matchstick-size pieces. In a large bowl toss together 3 cups thinly sliced napa cabbage, 1 cup fresh parsley leaves, 1 cup fresh mint leaves, the jicama, and the apple. In a small bowl whisk together ½ cup extra virgin olive oil, 2 tablespoons fresh orange juice, 2 tablespoons fresh lemon juice, and ½ teaspoon black pepper. Drizzle over salad; toss to coat.

GARLICKY LAMB AND
EGGPLANT LETTUCE BUNDLES

>> <<

MAKES 4 SERVINGS

1 pound ground lamb

1 medium eggplant, cut into ½- to
1-inch pieces

3 tablespoons extra virgin olive oil

2 cloves garlic, minced

1 teaspoon Mediterranean
Seasoning (recipe, page 296)

⅓ of a medium red onion, thinly
sliced

½ cup snipped fresh parsley

¼ cup coarsely chopped fresh mint

2 tablespoons fresh lemon juice

1 tablespoon red wine vinegar

2 heads Bibb lettuce

*Cut the eggplant fairly small—½- to 1-inch pieces—in order for it to blend well with
the ground lamb and be served neatly in the lettuce leaves.*

In a large skillet cook the ground lamb and eggplant in hot oil over medium-high heat 10 to 15 minutes or until the meat is browned and the eggplant is tender. Stir in garlic and Mediterranean Seasoning. Cook and stir 1 minute. Remove skillet from heat. Stir in onion, parsley, mint, lemon juice, and vinegar.

Separate the leaves from each head of lettuce. Spoon the lamb and eggplant filling into lettuce leaves.

Grilled Chicken and Zucchini
with Red Pepper Sauce,
recipe, page 167

POULTRY

The juicy texture and mild taste of chicken and turkey make these popular birds perfect palettes for flavor profiles from around the world—Mexican, Thai, Chinese, Caribbean, Moroccan, and Philippine—which you'll find in this chapter. From smoky grilled boneless breasts coated in Egyptian spices to crisp-skinned flash-roasted thighs, there is a poultry dish for every palate.

CHOOSING CHICKEN & TURKEY

Poultry is popular for its mild flavor, versatility, and how quickly it cooks. (See chart, opposite, for pieces that can be cooked in 30 minutes or less.) There are particular pieces of chicken and turkey that cook more quickly than others, of course. In general, bone-in pieces will take longer to cook than boneless. A boneless, skinless chicken breast that has been pounded to a ½- to ¼-inch thickness cooks in minutes. However, cooking bone-in poultry in a 30-minute recipe is still very doable.

Before you cook anything, though, you need to know how to get the best-quality poultry. Buy organic and free-range birds if you can, but if you don't have easy access to them, you still need to read labels. Nearly all of the poultry sold in supermarkets is "enhanced." This means that has been injected with saltwater to plump it up—sometimes up to 15% of its weight. This means that 4 ounces of enhanced chicken will contain as much as 400 milligrams of sodium—compared with 50 to 70 milligrams in untreated poultry. Because the salt has been injected into the flesh of the bird, there is no way to wash it off. And, due to a labeling loophole, these chickens can still be called "natural" or "all-natural." The only way to know if you are holding treated or untreated chicken is to read the label.

If possible, look at natural- and whole-foods stores, farmers markets, and local farmers for untreated poultry.

COOKING TIMES FOR POULTRY

CHICKEN

Skillet-Cooking
- Skinless, boneless breast halves (6 to 8 ounces): 15 to 18 minutes over medium heat, turning once
- Skinless, boneless thighs (3 to 4 ounces): 14 to 18 minutes over medium heat, turning once

Broiling
- Meaty pieces (bone-in breast, drumsticks, bone-in thighs): 25 to 30 minutes, turning once
- Skinless, boneless, chicken breast halves (6 to 8 ounces): 15 to 18 minutes, turning once

Grilling
- Skinless, boneless breast halves (6 to 8 ounces): 15 to 18 minutes over medium heat, turning once
- Skinless, boneless thighs (4 to 5 ounces): 12 to 15 minutes over medium heat, turning once
- Patties (¾ inch): 14 to 18 minutes over medium heat, turning once

TURKEY

Skillet Cooking
- Breast tenderloin steaks (½ inch thick, 4 to 6 ounces): 15 to 18 minutes on medium heat

Broiling
- Breast cutlet (2 ounces): 6 to 8 minutes, turning once
- Breast tenderloin steaks (½ inch thick, 4 to 6 ounces): 8 to 10 minutes, turning once

Grilling
- Turkey breast tenderloin (¾ to 1 inch thick, 8 to 10 ounces): 16 to 20 minutes over medium heat, turning once
- Patties (¾ inch): 14 to 18 minutes over medium heat, turning once

BUTTERFLYING A BIRD

Cooking a whole chicken can take far more than an hour. But there is a technique you can use to speed up this process considerably. It's not done in 30 minutes, but it is much faster than a whole bird. "Spatchcock" is an old term that describes the process of splitting a small bird—such as a chicken—down the back, then opening out and flattening the two sides like a book so that it cooks much more quickly than it would whole. It is similar to butterflying but refers only to fowl. To spatchcock a whole chicken, use kitchen shears to cut along both sides of the backbone. Remove the backbone. Turn the chicken, skin side up, and press down between the breasts to break the breast bone. Flatten it out. Rub with olive oil and sprinkle with the seasoning blend of your choice (see page 296). Grill, breast side down, over indirect or medium-high heat 10 to 15 minutes or until nicely charred. Flip and grill an additional 30 to 35 minutes or until the internal temperature reaches 165°F in the thickest part of the breast. Let rest 10 minutes. Serve with lemon wedges.

>> BASIC ROAST CHICKEN <<

MAKES 6 TO 8 SERVINGS
(5 TO 6 CUPS CHOPPED OR
SHREDDED CHICKEN)

1 4- to 5-pound whole chicken
1 tablespoon extra virgin olive oil
1 teaspoon black pepper
1 medium lemon, sliced
1 small bunch fresh herbs, such as
   parsley, rosemary, or thyme

While rotisserie chickens from your supermarket deli are a tempting convenience, they are likely injected with a saline solution to plump them up—and seasoned with additional salt as well. This herb- and lemon-roasted chicken is a delicious, Paleo-approved substitute for those supermarket birds. Look for a chicken that has not been injected with solution. Enjoy this as an entrée on its own or refrigerate it for use during the week.

Preheat oven to 425°F. Place rack in middle of oven. Remove neck and giblets from cavity of chicken (save for another use or discard). Drizzle chicken with oil and rub over skin. Sprinkle chicken inside and out with pepper. Place lemon slices and fresh herbs inside cavity. Place chicken, breast side up, in a roasting pan, oven-safe large frying pan, or cast-iron skillet. If desired, tie drumsticks together with 100%-cotton kitchen string.

Roast chicken, uncovered, 15 minutes. Reduce oven temperature to 375°F. Roast 50 to 60 minutes more or until juices run clear and a thermometer inserted into inner thigh (do not let thermometer touch bone) registers 165°F.

Let stand 15 to 20 minutes before carving. (Or let cool 30 minutes. Remove meat; discard skin and bones. Store in a tightly covered container in the refrigerator up to 4 days or freeze up to 3 months.)

CHICKEN CHOPPED SALAD
WITH MANGO-LIME DRESSING

>> <<

MAKES 2 SERVINGS

- 1 10-ounce package chopped romaine lettuce
- ½ of a large English cucumber, chopped
- 1 medium sweet pepper, seeded and chopped
- 1 avocado, halved, seeded, peeled, and chopped
- ¼ cup sliced scallions
- ½ cup unsalted roasted sunflower seeds
- 1½ cups shredded Basic Roast Chicken (recipe, page 152)
- ¾ cup Mango-Lime Salad Dressing (recipe, page 300)
  Black pepper

If you can't find packaged chopped romaine lettuce, it takes just a few minutes to chop up a small head of romaine lettuce, rinse the chopped lettuce, and spin it dry in a salad spinner. It's important that lettuce leaves are dry before tossing with dressing. If they're wet, the dressing won't cling to the leaves.

Place romaine lettuce in a large salad bowl. Arrange cucumber, sweet pepper, avocado, scallions, sunflower seeds, and chicken on lettuce.

Just before serving, drizzle salad with Mango-Lime Salad Dressing; toss to coat. Season to taste with black pepper.

SHAVED SPROUTS AND CHICKEN SALAD

>> <<

MAKES **4** SERVINGS

⅓ cup extra virgin olive oil

3 to 4 tablespoons fresh lemon juice

1½ to 2 teaspoons Dijon-Style Mustard (recipe, page 304)

1 9-ounce package shaved fresh Brussels sprouts

½ cup snipped fresh mint

2 cups shredded Basic Roast Chicken (recipe, page 152)

1 cup halved seedless red grapes

1 sweet-tart apple (such as Pink Lady), cored and diced

1 cup chopped pecans

This is the perfect salad for one of the first days of fall, when the weather is warm enough for a salad supper but cool enough that you might be craving autumnal flavors—apples, pecans, and peak-season Brussels sprouts.

In a large bowl whisk together olive oil, lemon juice, and Dijon-Style Mustard. Add Brussels sprouts and mint; toss to coat. Add chicken, grapes, apple, and pecans. Toss to combine.

CHICKEN WRAPS WITH
>> FIERY CITRUS SAUCE <<

MAKES 4 SERVINGS

½ cup finely chopped, seeded
   poblano chiles (tip, page 37)

¼ cup finely chopped, seeded
   serrano or jalapeño chile (tip,
   page 37)

3 cloves garlic, minced

2 tablespoons coconut oil

½ cup fresh orange juice

¼ cup unsulfured golden raisins

1 teaspoon Jamaican Jerk
   Seasoning (recipe, page 296)

⅛ teaspoon crushed red pepper
   (optional)

2 limes

2 cups shredded Basic Roast
   Chicken (recipe, page 152)

8 Bibb lettuce leaves

1 cup chopped cucumber

½ cup slivered red onion

¼ cup snipped fresh cilantro
   Lime wedges (optional)

*Two types of chiles—milder poblano and tiny but fiery serranos—give the sauce
for these wraps its spirited flavor. If you prefer a milder flavor, use jalapeño instead
of the serrano.*

In a medium skillet cook poblano and serrano chiles and the garlic in hot
coconut oil over medium heat 3 to 5 minutes or until chiles are tender,
stirring occasionally. Add orange juice, raisins, Jamaican Jerk Seasoning,
and, if desired, crushed red pepper. Bring to boiling; reduce heat. Boil gently,
uncovered, 3 to 5 minutes or until liquid is reduced by about half. Remove
from heat; cool 5 minutes.

Meanwhile, remove 1 teaspoon zest and squeeze ¼ cup juice from the limes.
Stir lime zest and juice and chicken into skillet.

Fill lettuce leaves with chicken mixture. Top with cucumber, red onion, and
cilantro. If desired, serve with lime wedges.

CURRIED MANGO-LIME CHICKEN SALAD

>>   <<

MAKES **4** SERVINGS

2 teaspoons extra virgin olive oil

½ cup slivered almonds

1 teaspoon salt-free mild curry powder

¼ cup Paleo Mayo (recipe, page 305)

¼ cup Mango-Lime Salad Dressing (recipe, page 300)

2 cups shredded Basic Roast Chicken (recipe, page 152)

¾ cup thinly sliced celery

¾ cup diced, peeled jicama

¾ cup diced English cucumber

¾ cup diced fresh pineapple

½ cup snipped fresh cilantro or mint

Bibb or romaine lettuce leaves

Many supermarket produce sections have prepared and cut-up fruit for convenience—most notably melons and pineapple. If you can find peeled and cored fresh pineapple or even chunks or rings, it will make dicing the pineapple for this recipe that much quicker.

———————————————

In a small skillet heat the olive oil over medium heat. Add almonds and curry powder; cook and stir until almonds are toasted and coated with curry powder. Remove to a large bowl.

Add Paleo Mayo and Mango-Lime Salad Dressing to nuts in bowl; stir well to infuse dressing with curry powder from the nuts. Add chicken, celery, jicama, cucumber, pineapple, and cilantro; stir gently to coat. Serve immediately or chill up to 1 day. Serve the salad on lettuce leaves.

>> SWEET-AND-SOUR CHICKEN <<

MAKES 4 SERVINGS

2   2-pound or one 4-pound
      spaghetti squash

1   medium green sweet pepper, cut
      into 1-inch pieces

½   cup coarsely chopped onion

1   tablespoon peeled and minced
      fresh ginger

4   cloves garlic, minced

2   teaspoons salt-free Chinese
      five-spice powder

1   cup purchased sliced carrots

2   tablespoons coconut oil

3   to 4 cups chopped Basic Roast
      Chicken (recipe, page 152)

1   cup cubed fresh pineapple

⅔   cup fresh orange juice

½   of a 6-ounce can no-salt-added
      tomato paste (⅓ cup)

⅓   cup red wine vinegar

2   teaspoons arrowroot

¼   cup unsweetened coconut
      chips, lightly toasted* (optional)

Missing take-out? This Paleo version of the popular dish is full of good-for-you veggies and a well-balanced sauce served on a bed of spaghetti squash. Next time try parsnip noodles (page 242) or cauliflower couscous (page 235).

Cut spaghetti squash in half crosswise. Scoop out seeds and strings. Pierce skins of squash halves in several places with a fork or sharp knife. Place squash halves, cut sides down, in a microwave-safe 2-quart baking dish. Cover with vented plastic wrap. Microwave 8 to 10 minutes or until squash is tender. Set aside to cool slightly.

Meanwhile, in a small bowl toss together sweet pepper, onion, ginger, garlic, and 1 teaspoon of the five-spice powder.

In a wok or extra-large skillet cook carrots in 1 tablespoon of the coconut oil over medium-high heat 3 minutes. Add sweet pepper and onion; cook and stir 3 to 4 minutes or until vegetables are crisp-tender. Add chicken and pineapple.

In a small bowl whisk together orange juice, tomato paste, vinegar, arrowroot, and the remaining 1 teaspoon five-spice powder until smooth. Add to wok. Cook and stir until sauce is slightly thickened.

Use a fork to scrape the squash into long shreds. Serve chicken and vegetables over squash. If desired, sprinkle with toasted coconut.

*Tip: To toast coconut, spread the coconut chips in a shallow baking pan. Bake in a 350°F oven 5 to 10 minutes or until light golden brown, shaking the pan once or twice.

Sesame-Almond Fried
Chicken with Tomato-Kale
Salad, recipe, page 162

SESAME-ALMOND FRIED CHICKEN WITH TOMATO-KALE SALAD

>>   <<

MAKES **4** SERVINGS

3 tablespoons sesame seeds

½ cup slivered almonds

1 tablespoon Cajun Seasoning (recipe, page 296)

2 eggs

3 tablespoons unsweetened almond milk or water

1½ pounds chicken breast tenderloins

3 tablespoons coconut oil

1 recipe Tomato-Kale Salad

These crispy and slightly spicy chicken fingers are delicious served naked or with a dipping sauce. Try Paleo Ketchup (page 304), BBQ Sauce (page 305), or, if you like even more heat, the Chipotle Paleo Mayo variation (page 305).

Preheat oven to 300°F. In a dry extra-large skillet toast sesame seeds over medium heat 1 to 2 minutes, shaking skillet occasionally. Transfer sesame seeds to a spice grinder; pulse until coarsely ground. Remove to a shallow dish. In the same skillet toast the almonds over medium heat 2 to 3 minutes, stirring occasionally. Transfer almonds to the spice grinder; pulse until coarsely ground. Remove to dish with sesame seeds. Add Cajun Seasoning; stir to combine.

In another shallow dish lightly beat eggs and almond milk to combine. Dip chicken tenderloins, a few at a time, in egg mixture, turning to coat. Allow excess to drip off. Dip in almond mixture, turning to coat.

Heat 2 tablespoons of the coconut oil in the extra-large skillet over medium heat. Cook half of the tenderloins in the hot oil, leaving a little space between the tenderloins, 6 to 8 minutes or until chicken is no longer pink, turning once halfway through cooking. Remove to a shallow baking pan. Keep warm in preheated oven. Repeat with remaining 1 tablespoon coconut oil and remaining tenderloins.

Serve chicken with Tomato-Kale Salad.

Tomato-Kale Salad: In a large bowl toss together 3 cups torn romaine lettuce, 2 cups kale cut into ribbons, and ⅓ cup Roasted Garlic Vinaigrette (recipe, page 300). Top with 1 avocado, seeded, peeled, and sliced; ½ cup halved red and/or yellow cherry tomatoes; and ⅓ cup slivered red onion. Drizzle with an additional 2 to 3 tablespoons Roasted Garlic Vinaigrette.

PAN-ROASTED CHICKEN
>> BREASTS WITH ARTICHOKES, <<
LEMON, AND ASPARAGUS

MAKES 4 SERVINGS

2 tablespoons extra virgin olive oil

4 skinless, boneless chicken
breast halves

1 leek, thinly sliced

2 cloves garlic, minced
Pinch crushed red pepper

¼ cup dry white wine

1 cup unsalted chicken stock

1 cup no-salt-added canned
artichoke hearts, quartered

1 pound fresh asparagus, trimmed
and cut into 1-inch pieces

2 to 3 tablespoons fresh lemon
juice

2 tablespoons snipped fresh
tarragon

This is a fitting dinner for spring, when asparagus is in season and is at its sweetest and most tender. If you can't find no-salt-added artichoke hearts, frozen artichoke hearts work well too. You might need to cook them the full 5 minutes to get them tender.

In a large skillet heat oil over medium-high heat. Add chicken; cook 5 minutes or until well browned on bottoms. Flip chicken; cook 3 minutes. Remove chicken to plate.

Add leek, garlic, and crushed red pepper to the skillet; cook and stir 3 to 5 minutes or until leek is softened. Add wine; cook until wine is reduced by half, stirring to scrape up crusty browned bits on bottom of skillet. Add stock and artichokes. Return chicken to skillet; arrange asparagus on top of chicken. Bring to boiling; reduce heat. Cover and simmer 3 to 5 minutes or until chicken is done (165°F).

Remove chicken, asparagus, and artichokes to serving plates. Stir lemon juice and tarragon into sauce in skillet; spoon over chicken and vegetables.

CHICKEN ADOBO WITH ORANGE AND WILTED SPINACH

>>   <<

MAKES **4** SERVINGS

1   14.5-ounce can no-salt-added diced tomatoes, drained

1   cup cider vinegar

3   cloves garlic, minced

1   teaspoon paprika

¼   teaspoon crushed red pepper

2   bay leaves

8   skinless, boneless chicken thighs

3   tablespoons extra virgin olive oil

¼   cup coarsely chopped onion

1   10-ounce package fresh baby spinach

1   large orange, peeled and sectioned (tip, page 114)

There are two basic types of adobo. The Mexican version features a dark red, thick sauce or paste made from ground chiles, herbs, and vinegar. This dish is closer to the Philippine version of adobo—a dish of meat or poultry that is marinated and cooked in a mixture of vinegar, garlic, herbs, spices, and sometimes coconut milk.

For sauce, in a large skillet stir together first six ingredients (through bay leaves). Add chicken, covering with sauce. Bring to boiling; reduce heat. Cover and simmer 8 minutes. Remove chicken and pat dry with paper towels; set aside. Increase heat to medium-high; cook 10 minutes or until the sauce is slightly reduced.

Meanwhile, in another large skillet heat 2 tablespoons of the olive oil over medium-high heat. Carefully add chicken and onion. Cook 4 minutes or until chicken is done (165°F), turning chicken once and stirring onion as needed to avoid burning. Remove chicken and onion; cover to keep warm. Add the remaining 1 tablespoon oil to skillet. Add spinach; cook over medium heat just until wilted. Stir in orange sections.

Remove bay leaves from the sauce and discard. Divide spinach among four plates; add chicken and onion. Spoon sauce over chicken.

ITALIAN CHICKEN CUTLETS
>> WITH WILTED KALE SALAD <<

MAKES 4 SERVINGS

1 bunch fresh kale, trimmed and
   coarsely torn
⅓ cup fresh lemon juice
4 skinless, boneless chicken
   breast halves
⅓ cup coconut flour
⅓ cup almond flour
2 to 3 tablespoons Mediterranean
   Seasoning (recipe, page 296)
1 to 2 teaspoons crushed red
   pepper
1 egg
1 tablespoon water
⅓ cup extra virgin olive oil
¼ cup walnut oil or extra virgin
   olive oil
½ cup chopped walnuts, toasted
   (tip, page 63)
2 medium shallots, very thinly sliced
2 cloves garlic, minced

It may sound silly to massage your salad greens, but in the case of kale, it makes perfect sense. Many kale salad recipes call for the leaves to be massaged for a few minutes before tossing them with other ingredients. Massaging kale breaks down the tough cellulose structure in the leaves, shrinking them and making them much more tender, silky, and sweet without cooking.

Place kale in a large bowl. Drizzle with lemon juice and massage into kale for 3 minutes or until kale slightly wilts.

Using the flat side of a meat mallet, flatten chicken between two pieces of plastic wrap to ¼ inch thick.

In a shallow dish combine coconut and almond flours, Mediterranean Seasoning, and crushed red pepper. In a second shallow dish whisk together egg and the water. Dip chicken into egg mixture, then into the flour mixture to coat.

In an extra-large skillet heat the ⅓ cup olive oil over medium heat. Add chicken to hot oil; cook 2 to 3 minutes per side or until golden, adding more oil if needed.

Drizzle kale with walnut oil. Add walnuts, shallots, and garlic; toss to mix. Serve with chicken.

GRILLED CHICKEN AND ZUCCHINI
WITH RED PEPPER SAUCE

>>   <<

MAKES **4** SERVINGS

1 small sweet red pepper

⅓ cup sliced almonds

4 6- to 8-ounce skinless, boneless
   chicken breast halves

1 teaspoon black pepper

2 tablespoons extra virgin olive oil

2 medium zucchini, halved
   lengthwise

¼ cup halved grape or cherry
   tomatoes

1 clove garlic

1 tablespoon red wine vinegar

1 teaspoon smoked paprika

   Sliced fresh basil leaves (optional)

The sauce for this simple grilled chicken and vegetable dish is a simplified version of romesco, a sauce of red peppers, tomatoes, onion, garlic, almonds, and olive oil that originated in Catalonia, Spain. It's wonderful on either grilled poultry or fish.

Preheat broiler to high. Line a shallow baking pan with foil. Cut the four sides of the sweet pepper away from the seeds and stem. Place pepper pieces, cut sides down, in the prepared pan. Broil 4 to 6 inches from heat 6 to 8 minutes or until blackened. Wrap pepper pieces tightly in foil. Let stand 15 minutes. When cool enough to handle, gently peel the blackened skin off of the peppers.

Meanwhile, in a small dry skillet toast almonds over medium-low heat 2 to 4 minutes or until fragrant and lightly browned.

Sprinkle chicken with ½ teaspoon of the black pepper. Brush cut sides of zucchini with 1 tablespoon of the olive oil; sprinkle with ¼ teaspoon of the black pepper.

Grill chicken and zucchini over medium heat 8 minutes or until chicken is done (165°F) and zucchini is tender and browned, turning once halfway through grilling. (Or grill chicken and zucchini on a stove-top grill pan over medium heat.) If desired, chop zucchini.

Meanwhile, for red pepper sauce, in a food processor or blender combine the sweet pepper pieces, toasted almonds, tomatoes, garlic, vinegar, paprika, the remaining 1 tablespoon olive oil, and the remaining ¼ teaspoon black pepper. Pulse until smooth.

Sprinkle grilled chicken and zucchini with additional black pepper. Serve with red pepper sauce sprinkled, if desired, with fresh basil.

3 WAYS
WITH BUTTERNUT
SQUASH CUBES

Butternut squash is so versatile. It can be steamed or roasted and pureed, roasted in chunks or wedges until it's caramelized, stirred into a stew, and turned into a smooth and creamy soup. In its whole state, it can be a bit daunting to break it down, scoop the seeds, and then cut it into the necessary size for the recipe you are making—and make the recipe—in 30 minutes or less. Fortunately, precubed butternut squash is now available in both fresh and frozen forms. The freezing process does break down some of the fibers—making the frozen product softer than the fresh product—so keep that in mind as you decide which to buy. Precut cubes are used in Quick Chipotle Chicken-Butternut Squash Chili (page 169), Wilted Spinach Salad with Roasted Butternut Squash and Chicken (page 170), and Smoky Chicken-Squash Cabbage Tacos with Quick Salsa (page 171).

QUICK CHIPOTLE CHICKEN-BUTTERNUT SQUASH CHILI

>>   <<

MAKES **4** SERVINGS

1   pound ground uncooked chicken

⅓   cup finely chopped onion

2   tablespoons extra virgin olive oil

4   cups precut butternut squash cubes

1   cup chopped green sweet pepper

1   tablespoon salt-free chili powder

1   teaspoon ground chipotle chile pepper

2   cups unsalted chicken stock

1   14.5-ounce can no-salt-added diced tomatoes

     Snipped fresh cilantro

     Pepitas

If you can find precut butternut squash in the fresh produce section, use that instead of the frozen product in this quick-simmering chili. It will hold its shape better.

In a Dutch oven cook ground chicken and onion in hot oil 5 minutes or until lightly browned. Stir in butternut squash, sweet pepper, chili powder, and ground chipotle chile pepper. Cook 2 more minutes or just until pepper is softened, stirring occasionally.

Stir in stock and undrained tomatoes. Bring to boiling; reduce heat. Cover and simmer 10 to 15 minutes or until squash is tender. Sprinkle servings with cilantro and pepitas.

WILTED SPINACH SALAD
>> WITH ROASTED BUTTERNUT SQUASH <<
AND CHICKEN

MAKES **4** SERVINGS

4 cups precut butternut squash cubes

1 to 1¼ pounds skinless, boneless chicken breast halves

2 tablespoons extra virgin olive oil

2 teaspoons Mediterranean Seasoning (recipe, page 296)

1 6- to 8-ounce package fresh spinach

1 shallot, thinly sliced

¼ to ½ cup Roasted Garlic Vinaigrette (recipe, page 300)

¼ cup chopped walnuts

The heat from the hot chicken and squash just barely wilts the spinach in this colorful salad. A sprinkling of walnuts over the top adds crunch.

Preheat oven to 450°F. Line a large baking sheet with parchment paper or foil. In a medium bowl toss butternut squash and chicken breasts with the olive oil and Mediterranean Seasoning; arrange in a single layer on the prepared baking sheet. Roast 20 minutes or until squash is tender and chicken is done (165°F).

Meanwhile, on a large platter or in a salad bowl combine spinach, shallot, and ¼ cup of the Roasted Garlic Vinaigrette. Thinly slice chicken breasts. Arrange hot squash and chicken on spinach. Sprinkle with walnuts. If desired, drizzle with additional Roasted Garlic Vinaigrette.

SMOKY CHICKEN-
>> SQUASH CABBAGE TACOS <<
WITH QUICK SALSA

MAKES **4** SERVINGS

4 **cups precut butternut squash cubes**

2 **tablespoons extra virgin olive oil**

2 **cups shredded Basic Roast Chicken (recipe, page 152)**

2 **14.5-ounce cans no-salt-added diced tomatoes**

2 **tablespoons fresh lime juice**

2 **teaspoons Mexican Seasoning (recipe, page 296)**

1 **teaspoon smoked paprika**

1 **cup fresh cilantro leaves, lightly packed**

2 **fresh jalapeño chiles, quartered (tip, page 37)**

2 **cloves garlic, smashed**

Red cabbage leaves

This recipe makes a little bit more salsa than you'll need for the tacos, but it's convenient to have extra salsa on hand. Serve leftover salsa with veggie chips or spoon it over scrambled or fried eggs.

In a large skillet cook squash in hot oil over medium heat 10 minutes or until almost tender, stirring occasionally. Stir in chicken, 1 can undrained tomatoes, the lime juice, Mexican Seasoning, and paprika. Bring to boiling; reduce heat. Cover and simmer 5 minutes. Uncover and simmer 5 minutes more.

Meanwhile, for the salsa, in a food processor or blender combine the remaining undrained tomatoes, the cilantro, jalapeños, and garlic. Cover and process or blend until very finely chopped.

Spoon chicken, squash, and sauce into cabbage leaves. Top with the salsa. Cut in half to serve. Store any leftover salsa in the refrigerator up to 1 week.

DRIED APRICOT-STUFFED
>> CHICKEN BREASTS WITH ROASTED <<
CAULIFLOWER

MAKES **4** SERVINGS

⅓ cup coarsely chopped unsulfured dried apricots

¼ cup boiling water

2 tablespoons coarsely chopped pecans or cashews, toasted (tip, page 63)

1 tablespoon dry sherry

4 cups cauliflower florets

3 tablespoons extra virgin olive oil

½ teaspoon black pepper

2 cloves garlic, minced

1 teaspoon fresh thyme leaves

4 6- to 8-ounce boneless, skinless chicken breast halves

½ teaspoon Smoky Seasoning (see recipe, page 296)

Cracked black pepper

Snipped fresh thyme

This recipe is yet another example of the smart use of the microwave to partially cook vegetables quickly and then finish them in the oven (or in a grill) to brown the exterior for savory flavor and a crisp-tender texture.

Preheat oven to 400°F. Place apricots in a small bowl; pour the boiling water over apricots and let stand 3 minutes. In a blender combine apricots and any liquid, the nuts, and sherry. Cover and blend until a chunky paste forms.

In a large microwave-safe bowl toss cauliflower with 2 tablespoons of the olive oil and ¼ teaspoon of the pepper. Microwave, covered, 2 minutes. Stir in garlic. Transfer cauliflower to a foil-lined baking sheet; bake 10 minutes or until tender and lightly browned. Sprinkle with fresh thyme. Cover to keep warm.

Using a sharp knife, cut a pocket in each chicken breast half by cutting horizontally through the thickest portion to, but not through, the other side. Spoon apricot mixture into each pocket, using large toothpicks or small skewers as needed to secure openings. Combine the remaining 1 tablespoon oil, the remaining ¼ teaspoon pepper, and the Smoky Seasoning; brush over chicken breasts.

Heat an oven-going skillet over medium-high heat; add chicken breasts and brown quickly on all sides (add additional oil if needed to keep chicken from sticking to the pan). Cover skillet loosely with foil and carefully transfer to the oven; bake 5 minutes or until done (165° F). Sprinkle cauliflower with cracked black pepper and additional thyme; serve with chicken.

GRILLED ZA'ATAR CHICKEN AND VEGETABLES

>> <<

MAKES 2 SERVINGS

1 teaspoon ground sumac

1 tablespoon dried thyme

1 teaspoon sesame seeds, toasted
  (tip, page 69)

1 medium zucchini, sliced

1 medium yellow sweet pepper,
  seeded and sliced

1 small white or red onion, cut
  into wedges

3 tablespoons extra virgin olive oil

2 6- to 8-ounce skinless, boneless
  chicken breast halves

  Lemon wedges

1 recipe Cashew Cream (recipe,
  page 304) (optional)

  Sesame seeds, toasted (optional)

Za'atar is an herb and spice blend used in Arabic cooking that is made up of dried oregano, thyme, and savory, as well as sesame seeds and dried sumac. Commercial versions usually contain salt as well. While it may be unfamiliar to most Americans as a flavoring, ground sumac is used widely in Middle Eastern cooking. The dark red spice is made from the dried berries of a bush of the same name and has a fruity, astringent flavor. Look for it at specialty spice stores or Middle Eastern markets.

For za'atar seasoning, in a spice grinder combine sumac, thyme, and the 1 teaspoon toasted sesame seeds. Process until finely ground.

In a medium bowl combine zucchini, sweet pepper, and onion. Drizzle vegetables with 2 tablespoons of the oil and sprinkle with 2 teaspoons of the za'atar seasoning. Stir well to coat vegetables.

Using the flat side of a meat mallet, flatten chicken between two pieces of plastic wrap to about ¾ inch thick. Brush chicken with the remaining 1 tablespoon olive oil and sprinkle with the remaining za'atar seasoning.

Grill chicken, covered, over medium heat 8 to 10 minutes or until no longer pink, turning once halfway through cooking. Grill vegetables alongside chicken for 6 to 8 minutes or until crisp-tender, turning once. (Or grill chicken on a stove-top grill pan over medium-high heat. Remove chicken; cover to keep warm. Grill vegetables over medium-high heat.)

Serve chicken with vegetables and lemon wedges. If desired, top with Cashew Cream and sprinkle with additional toasted sesame seeds.

CILANTRO-CHICKEN COLLARD GREEN ENCHILADAS

>> <<

MAKES 4 SERVINGS

8 collard green leaves

⅓ cup finely chopped onion

3 tablespoons extra virgin olive oil

2 cloves garlic, minced

1 6-ounce can no-salted-added tomato paste

2 tablespoons ground ancho chile pepper or salt-free chili powder

1 teaspoon dried oregano

1 teaspoon ground cumin

2 cups unsalted chicken stock

½ cup carrot juice

2 tablespoons fresh lemon juice

3 cups shredded Basic Roast Chicken (recipe, page 152) or other cooked chicken

1 cup chopped fresh cilantro

½ cup chopped scallions

¾ cup Cashew Cream (recipe, page 304)

2 teaspoons Mexican Seasoning (recipe, page 296)

These clever skillet enchiladas are made by rolling up a creamy and flavorful chicken filling into sturdy collard leaves that have been blanched so they cook quickly in an aromatic sauce made with tomato paste, ancho chile, onion, garlic, chicken stock, and a surprising splash of carrot juice.

Bring a large pot of water to boiling. Fill a large bowl with ice water. Trim the stem from each collard leaf. Working with 3 or 4 leaves at a time, blanch the leaves in the boiling water 30 seconds or just until softened. Immediately plunge leaves into the ice water to cool. Drain leaves in a colander.

For sauce, in an extra-large skillet cook onion in hot oil 5 minutes or until tender. Add garlic; cook 30 seconds. Stir in tomato paste, ground ancho chile pepper, oregano, and cumin. Cook and stir 1 minute. Gradually whisk in chicken stock, carrot juice, and lemon juice. Bring to a simmer, stirring occasionally.

For filling, in a large bowl combine the shredded chicken, cilantro, scallions, Cashew Cream, and Mexican Seasoning. Spoon about ½ cup of the filling on each collard leaf. Roll up leaves.

Place enchiladas in the sauce. Cover and simmer 10 minutes or until heated through, gently shaking the skillet occasionally to prevent sticking.

If desired, sprinkle enchiladas with additional cilantro and drizzle with additional Cashew Cream.

>> LOADED BBQ CHICKEN NACHOS <<

4 medium sweet potatoes (about
   2 pounds), cut lengthwise into
   ¼-inch strips

3 tablespoons extra virgin olive oil

2 ripe avocados

2 tablespoons fresh lime juice

1 tablespoon minced shallot

1 clove garlic, minced

3 cups Basic Roast Chicken (recipe,
   page 152) or other cooked
   chicken

1½ cups BBQ Sauce (recipe,
   page 305)

1 ripe tomato, seeded and chopped

1 fresh jalapeño chile, seeded if
   desired and finely chopped (tip,
   page 37)

¼ cup chopped scallions

½ cup chopped fresh cilantro or
   parsley

This recipe is proof positive that you don't have to give up "fun foods" on the Paleo diet. Shredded cooked chicken is tossed with BBQ sauce, then layered on oven-baked sweet potato fries along with a quick fresh guacamole, tomato, scallions, and cilantro.

Preheat oven to 450°F.

For the sweet potato fries, in a large bowl combine sweet potatoes and the olive oil; toss to coat. Line two baking sheets with foil; brush foil with additional olive oil. Arrange sweet potatoes in a single layer on prepared baking sheets (do not crowd slices). Bake 10 minutes. Turn on broiler; broil fries for 3 to 5 minutes or until tender and brown around the edges.

Meanwhile, for the guacamole, halve and seed avocados; scoop out flesh and place in bowl. Stir in lime juice, shallot, and garlic.

In a microwave-safe bowl combine chicken and BBQ Sauce. Cover with vented plastic wrap and microwave 2 minutes or until chicken is hot, stirring once or twice.

Top sweet potato fries with BBQ chicken, guacamole, tomato, jalapeño, scallions, and cilantro.

THAI CHICKEN AND VEGETABLE STIR-FRY

>>   <<

MAKES **4** TO **6** SERVINGS

2 tablespoons coconut oil

1 pound skinless, boneless chicken breasts, cut into bite-size strips

1 large red sweet pepper, seeded and cut into bite-size strips

1 red onion, cut into thin wedges

4 scallions, cut into 1-inch pieces

1 stalk lemongrass, tough outer leaves removed, bruised with the back of a large knife, and tender core thinly sliced

1 3-inch piece ginger, peeled and minced

2 Thai chiles or 1 jalapeño chile, seeded if desired and finely chopped (tip, page 37)

2 cloves garlic, minced

2 baby bok choy, halved and sliced crosswise into 1-inch pieces

½ cup unsweetened pineapple juice

1 lime

½ cup Thai basil, torn

¼ cup coarsely chopped cilantro (optional)

Lime slices (optional)

Cook the bok choy for a maximum of 2 minutes to keep it bright green with a fresh taste and crisp texture. It can get overcooked very quickly.

In a large skillet heat 1 tablespoon of the coconut oil over medium-high heat. Add the chicken in a single layer and cook, without stirring, until browned, about 4 minutes. Use a metal spatula to flip chicken; cook, without stirring, just until chicken begins to color, about 3 minutes (chicken might not be cooked through). Remove chicken.

Add the remaining 1 tablespoon coconut oil to the skillet. Cook sweet pepper, onion, and scallions in hot oil 3 minutes or just until tender, stirring occasionally. Push vegetables to side of skillet. Add lemongrass, ginger, chiles, and garlic to skillet. Cook 2 minutes or until very fragrant, stirring frequently.

Return chicken and any accumulated juices to the skillet. Add bok choy and pineapple juice. Stir to combine all ingredients in skillet. Cover and cook 2 minutes or until chicken is cooked through and bok choy is tender.

Remove zest from lime and squeeze juice. Stir lime zest and juice, basil, and, if desired, cilantro into stir-fry. If desired, serve with lime slices.

CHICKEN TAGINE WITH SWEET POTATOES AND SQUASH

>>   <<

MAKES 4 TO 6 SERVINGS

2 tablespoons extra virgin olive oil
6 skinless, boneless chicken thighs (about 2 pounds)
2 cups chopped red onions
4 cloves garlic, thinly sliced
4 cinnamon sticks
2 bay leaves
1 10-ounce package frozen diced sweet potatoes
1 10-ounce package frozen diced butternut squash
2 large tomatoes, coarsely chopped
2 cups unsalted chicken stock
5 cups coarsely chopped, trimmed kale
1 teaspoon freshly ground black pepper
½ cup fresh cilantro leaves
½ cup fresh parsley leaves
¼ cup coarsely chopped fresh mint
1 cup roasted unsalted cashews

Tagine refers to a Moroccan dish of meat (usually chicken) and vegetables braised in spices and the conical pot in which it is cooked. Most authentic tagines (the pot) need to be soaked in water before being used the first time over a stove-top flame (and with a heat diffuser) because they are made of clay. An authentic tagine creates a cooking environment particularly suited to turning out very tender and moist meat, but a Dutch oven does the trick almost equally well.

In a 4- to 6-quart Dutch oven heat oil over medium-high heat. Add the chicken in a single layer and cook, without stirring, until browned, about 5 minutes. Use a metal spatula to flip chicken and cook, without stirring, until browned, about 3 minutes. Remove chicken to a plate.

Add onions, garlic, cinnamon sticks, and bay leaves to the Dutch oven. Cook about 4 minutes or until onions are translucent and beginning to color, stirring occasionally.

Stir in sweet potatoes, squash, tomatoes, and stock. Nestle the chicken thighs into the vegetable mixture; add any juices that accumulated on the plate. Add kale and sprinkle with pepper. Cover and cook about 5 minutes or until kale wilts. Stir in cilantro and parsley.

Ladle into bowls and top with mint and cashews. Serve immediately.

CHICKEN SALAD WITH
>> ROASTED GARLIC VINAIGRETTE <<

4 skinless, boneless chicken thighs

½ teaspoon freshly ground black
    pepper

4 cups purchased fresh broccoli
    florets

2 tablespoons extra virgin olive oil

1 8-ounce package sliced fresh
    mushrooms

1 large clove garlic, minced

1 tablespoon fresh lemon juice

6 cups torn romaine

4 Perfectly Steamed Hard-Cooked
    Eggs (recipe, page 256),
    thinly sliced

1 cup halved cherry tomatoes
    Freshly ground black pepper

½ cup Roasted Garlic Vinaigrette
    (recipe, page 300)

This chunky salad is a bit like a chicken Caesar salad with a lot of extra good stuff in it—broccoli, mushrooms, cherry tomatoes, and thinly sliced hard-cooked eggs. The broccoli and mushrooms are cooked in garlic before being tossed with the other ingredients. The cool, crisp greens and warm veggies are wonderful together.

Sprinkle chicken with the ½ teaspoon pepper. Grill chicken, covered, over medium heat 12 to 14 minutes or until done (165°F), turning once halfway through grilling. (Or grill chicken on a stove-top grill pan over medium heat.) Let stand 5 minutes. Thinly slice chicken.

Meanwhile, preheat an extra-large skillet over medium-high heat. Add broccoli; cook 10 minutes or until blistered on all sides, turning occasionally. Add oil, mushrooms, and garlic to skillet. Cover and cook 5 minutes or just until vegetables are tender and lightly charred. Drizzle with lemon juice.

Place romaine in an extra-large bowl. Top with broccoli, mushrooms, hard-cooked egg slices, tomatoes, and chicken. Sprinkle salad with freshly ground black pepper and drizzle with Roasted Garlic Vinaigrette; gently toss to combine.

ROASTED CHICKEN
>> AND VEGETABLES WITH <<
PORT WINE SAUCE

MAKES **4** SERVINGS

8 small bone-in chicken thighs
   (2 to 2 ½ pounds total)

4 cloves garlic, minced

1 teaspoon freshly ground
   black pepper

¼ teaspoon ground nutmeg

3 cups Brussels sprouts, halved

2 cups purchased sliced fresh
   cremini mushrooms

1 medium onion, cut into thin
   wedges

3 tablespoons extra virgin olive oil

1 tablespoon snipped fresh thyme

4 clusters red or green seedless
   grapes

1 cup port wine

2 sprigs fresh thyme

   Snipped fresh thyme (optional)

While port wine does have a fair amount of natural sugar in it—and it's not something you should sit and sip if you are trying to stick to eating Paleo—a little bit of reduced port wine drizzled over your dinner as a sauce is fine once in a while.

Adjust oven racks to lower one-third and upper one-third of oven. Preheat oven to 450°F. Loosen skin from the chicken thighs by running your finger under the skin (do not remove the skin). Spoon garlic under the skin; spread evenly over the meat. In a 15×10×1-inch baking pan arrange chicken thighs in a single layer. Sprinkle with ½ teaspoon of the pepper and the nutmeg. Roast 10 minutes.

Meanwhile, in an extra-large roasting pan combine Brussels sprouts, mushrooms, and onions. Drizzle vegetables with 2 tablespoons of the olive oil and sprinkle with the snipped thyme; toss to coat. Add to the pan with the chicken. Roast 10 minutes.

Gently toss grape clusters with the remaining 1 tablespoon olive oil. Add to pan with chicken. Roast 5 minutes more or until chicken is done (175°F) and vegetables are crisp-tender.

For port wine sauce, in a small saucepan bring wine and thyme sprigs to boiling; reduce heat. Boil gently, uncovered, 5 to 10 minutes or until reduced to about ⅓ cup. Discard thyme sprigs.

Arrange chicken, vegetables, and grapes on serving plates. Drizzle with port wine sauce. If desired, sprinkle with additional snipped fresh thyme.

Chicken and Mushroom Ramen, recipe, page 186

CHICKEN AND
>> MUSHROOM RAMEN <<

MAKES **4** SERVINGS

1 medium zucchini

4 skinless, boneless chicken thighs

1 teaspoon salt-free Chinese
   five-spice powder

½ teaspoon black pepper

8 cups unsalted chicken stock

1 1-inch piece ginger, peeled and
   cut into matchstick-size pieces

2 cloves garlic, peeled and thinly
   sliced

4 ounces shiitake mushrooms,
   stems removed and sliced

5 ounces fresh baby spinach,
   roughly chopped

2 Perfectly Steamed Hard-Cooked
   Eggs (recipe, page 256), halved
   lengthwise

   Sliced scallions

   Crushed red pepper (optional)

This warming, aromatic bowl of goodness proves that even Paleo enthusiasts can enjoy a big soupy bowl of Asian-style noodles. This noodle bowl is so fresh and delicious, you won't miss the grain-based variety a bit.

To make zucchini noodles, use a julienne slicer or spiralizer to cut zucchini into thin slices. Set zucchini noodles aside.

Preheat broiler. Rub chicken thighs with five-spice powder; sprinkle with black pepper. Place chicken thighs on a foil-lined baking sheet. Broil 4 to 5 inches from the heat 8 to 10 minutes or until done (175°F), turning once halfway through broiling. Let stand 10 minutes. Slice chicken and set aside.

Meanwhile, in a large saucepan combine stock, ginger, and garlic. Bring to boiling; reduce heat. Add mushrooms; simmer, uncovered, 2 minutes. Add zucchini noodles; simmer 1 minute. Remove saucepan from heat. Add spinach; stir just until wilted. Stir in chicken.

Divide among four bowls; top with hard-cooked egg halves and scallions. If desired, sprinkle with crushed red pepper.

CHICKEN AND BROCCOLI STIR-FRY

>> <<

MAKES **4** SERVINGS

1½ pounds skinless, boneless chicken thighs

1 teaspoon black pepper

3 tablespoons coconut oil

1 medium onion, halved lengthwise and sliced

1 8-ounce package sliced fresh mushrooms

1 12-ounce package fresh broccoli florets

2 tablespoons minced fresh ginger

3 cloves garlic, minced

2 tablespoons Lemon-Herb Seasoning (recipe, page 296)

¼ cup unsalted chicken stock

¼ cup apple cider

2 tablespoons sherry vinegar or white wine vinegar

½ cup chopped fresh cilantro

½ cup unsalted sliced or slivered almonds, toasted (tip, page 63)

This recipe calls for skinless, boneless chicken thighs, but you could substitute boneless, skinless chicken breast if you like.

Cut chicken into 1-inch pieces; sprinkle with pepper. In an extra-large skillet heat 1 tablespoon of the coconut oil over medium-high heat. Add half of the chicken; cook and stir 3 to 4 minutes or until no longer pink. Remove chicken to a bowl. Repeat with the remaining chicken and 1 tablespoon oil. Remove all chicken to the bowl; cover to keep warm.

In the same skillet heat the remaining 1 tablespoon oil. Add onion; cook and stir 2 minutes. Add mushrooms; cook and stir 2 minutes. Add broccoli; cook and stir 2 to 3 minutes or until vegetables are crisp-tender. Add ginger, garlic, and Lemon-Herb Seasoning; cook and stir 1 minute more. Remove vegetables from wok.

Add chicken stock, apple cider, and vinegar to skillet. Bring to boiling; boil to reduce slightly. Return chicken and vegetables to skillet; heat through. Stir in cilantro and almonds. Serve immediately.

MEXICAN CHICKEN
>> STUFFED PEPPERS <<

MAKES 4 SERVINGS

2 tablespoons extra virgin olive oil

½ cup chopped onion

4 cloves garlic, minced

1 medium jalapeño or serrano chile, seeded and chopped (tip, page 37)

2 pounds ground uncooked chicken or turkey

2 tablespoons Mexican Seasoning (recipe, page 296)

1 14.5 ounce can no-salt-added fire-roasted diced tomatoes

½ cup chopped fresh cilantro

4 medium red, yellow, and/or orange sweet peppers

Lime wedges

Blanching the pepper halves in boiling water for a couple minutes keeps them crisp enough to hold the hearty filling but soft enough to eat—without having to bake them in the oven.

In a large skillet heat oil over medium heat. Add onion, garlic, and chile; cook and stir 2 minutes. Add ground chicken; cook until no longer pink. Sprinkle with Mexican Seasoning; stir well. Stir in undrained tomatoes. Bring to boiling; reduce heat. Simmer, uncovered, 5 to 7 minutes or until most of the liquid has evaporated. Stir in ¼ cup of the cilantro.

Meanwhile, cut sweet peppers in half vertically (from stems to bottoms). Remove and discard stems, seeds, and membranes. In a large pot blanch peppers in boiling water 2 to 3 minutes or just until tender; drain. Fill peppers with chicken mixture.

For each serving, arrange 2 pepper halves on a plate. Sprinkle with the remaining cilantro and serve with lime wedges.

BBQ DRUMSTICKS
>> WITH FRUITY SLAW <<

MAKES 4 SERVINGS

8   chicken drumsticks (2 to
    2½ pounds total)

1   tablespoon Smoky Seasoning
    (recipe, page 296)

¾   cup BBQ Sauce (recipe,
    page 305)

1   14-ounce package coleslaw mix

¾   cup sliced scallions

½   cup fresh parsley leaves, chopped

¾   cup Paleo Mayo (recipe,
    page 305)

1   tablespoon fresh lemon juice
    Freshly ground black pepper

2   peaches, peeled, pitted, and
    sliced

Make this dish when peaches are at peak season—mid-July to early September (at the latest)—when they are so perfectly sweet and ripe that the juice runs down your chin if you eat one out of hand. It's a narrow window to enjoy such a delightful food, but it really is the only time to buy peaches.

Preheat broiler. Arrange drumsticks on a rimmed baking sheet lined with foil. Sprinkle drumsticks with Smoky Seasoning. Broil 6 to 8 inches from heat 15 minutes. Turn drumsticks over; broil about 10 minutes more or until chicken is done (175°F), brushing with BBQ Sauce the last 5 minutes of broiling.

Meanwhile, for fruity slaw, in a large bowl combine coleslaw mix, scallions, parsley, Paleo Mayo, and lemon juice. Season to taste with pepper. Gently stir in peaches.

Serve chicken with fruity slaw and, if desired, additional BBQ Sauce.

TURKEY-SPINACH BURGERS WITH TOMATO-CANTALOUPE SALSA

>>   <<

MAKES **4** SERVINGS

1 egg, lightly beaten

½ of a 10-ounce package frozen chopped spinach, thawed and well drained

⅓ cup finely chopped onion

1 tablespoon Mediterranean Seasoning (recipe, page 296)

1 pound uncooked ground turkey

1 tablespoon extra virgin olive oil

1 cup chopped cherry tomatoes

1 cup chopped cantaloupe

2 tablespoons snipped fresh cilantro

4 cups mixed greens

¼ cup Bright Citrus Vinaigrette (recipe, page 300)

2 tablespoons sliced almonds, toasted (tip, page 63)

Thawed chopped frozen spinach gives these turkey burgers color and a nutritional boost. (Squeeze it as dry as you can before working it into the meat mixture.) Use the remaining half in scrambled eggs or a smoothie the next morning.

In a large bowl combine egg, spinach, onion, and Mediterranean Seasoning. Add turkey; mix well. Shape turkey mixture into four patties. In a large skillet heat oil over medium-high heat. Add patties; reduce heat to medium. Cook patties 12 to 14 minutes or until done (165°F), turning once halfway through cooking.

Meanwhile, for salsa, in a medium bowl combine tomatoes, cantaloupe, and cilantro.

For salad, in a large bowl combine greens and Bright Citrus Vinaigrette. Sprinkle with almonds and toss to combine.

Top patties with salsa and serve with salad.

>> QUICK CHICKEN DUMPLING STEW <<

MAKES **4** SERVINGS

1 pound skinless, boneless chicken thighs, cut into bite-size pieces

2 tablespoons coconut oil

4 cloves garlic, minced

2 teaspoons paprika

1½ cups frozen mirepoix blend vegetables (chopped onion, celery, and carrots)

6 cups unsalted chicken stock

1 teaspoon dried thyme, crushed

½ teaspoon dried sage, crushed

2 cups torn trimmed fresh kale

2 cups frozen broccoli, cauliflower, and carrots vegetable blend

1 egg

2 tablespoons extra virgin olive oil

½ teaspoon granulated garlic

1 teaspoon Lemon-Herb Seasoning (recipe, page 296)

½ teaspoon black pepper

¾ cup arrowroot

⅔ cup almond meal

1 cup unsweetened almond milk

Dumplings fit into a Paleo diet when they're made from a seasoned blend of arrowroot, almond meal, and egg. They add a nice chewy element to this rich and homey stew.

In a 4- to 6-quart Dutch oven cook chicken in hot coconut oil over medium-high heat just until browned. Stir in minced garlic and paprika; add mirepoix vegetables. Cook 3 minutes more, stirring occasionally.

Add stock, thyme, and sage to Dutch oven. Bring to boiling; reduce heat. Cover and simmer 5 minutes. Add kale and frozen broccoli, cauliflower, and carrots; cover and simmer 5 minutes more.

Meanwhile, for dumplings, in a small bowl beat together egg, olive oil, granulated garlic, Lemon-Herb Seasoning, and black pepper. Stir in arrowroot and almond meal just until combined. Lightly dust a work surface with additional almond meal. On prepared surface roll out dumpling dough to a square about ¼ inch thick. Cut into 1-inch squares (dumplings do not have to be perfect squares).

Drop the dumplings into the hot stew. Cook 5 minutes, stirring occasionally. Add almond milk to stew; cook 1 to 2 minutes more or until heated through.

GRILLED TURKEY PAILLARDS WITH TOMATO AND ARUGULA SALAD

>>   <<

MAKES **4** SERVINGS

2 8- to 12-ounce turkey breast tenderloins

1 tablespoon dried oregano, crushed

1 tablespoon dried basil, crushed

1 tablespoon garlic powder or granulated garlic

1 tablespoon onion powder

2½ teaspoons freshly ground black pepper

1 teaspoon dried thyme, crushed

2 tablespoons extra virgin olive oil

2 cups grape or cherry tomatoes, halved

1 small Vidalia onion, halved and thinly sliced

½ cup extra virgin olive oil

1 tablespoon fresh lemon juice

2 teaspoons red wine vinegar

1 clove garlic, minced

4 cups baby arugula

½ cup fresh basil leaves, torn

½ cup fresh parsley leaves

A paillard is a fancy French name for a thin piece of meat or poultry that can be grilled or sautéed in minutes—perfect for when you're looking to make a super quick dinner.

Cut each turkey tenderloin horizontally in half. Using a meat mallet, flatten turkey between two pieces of plastic wrap to ¼ inch thick. In a small bowl combine oregano, basil, garlic powder, onion powder, the 2 teaspoons pepper, and the thyme. Rub the turkey with the 2 tablespoons olive oil. Sprinkle spice mixture on both sides of turkey pieces; rub into turkey.

For the salad, in a large bowl combine tomatoes, onion, the ½ cup olive oil, the lemon juice, vinegar, minced garlic, and the remaining ½ teaspoon pepper. Stir to coat. Let stand to blend flavors while the turkey is grilling.

Grill turkey, uncovered, over medium heat about 6 minutes or until no longer pink, turning once halfway through grilling. (Or cook turkey on a stove-top grill pan over medium heat.)

Add arugula, basil, and parsley to the salad; toss to mix. Serve turkey with salad.

>> CAJUN TURKEY WRAPS <<

MAKES 4 WRAPS

¼ cup extra virgin olive oil

2 medium red and/or yellow sweet
   peppers, seeded and cut into
   bite-size strips

1 medium onion, thinly sliced

2 8-ounce turkey breast
   tenderloins, cut into strips

1 to 2 tablespoons Cajun
   Seasoning (recipe, page 296)

4 coconut wraps

2 cups packaged fresh baby
   spinach

½ cup Paleo Aïoli (recipe,
   page 305)

Coconut wraps can dry out if they're not stored properly. Wrap leftover wraps tightly in plastic wrap and store them in a resealable plastic bag in the refrigerator. Bring to room temperature before trying to roll up—and do not freeze, which can cause them to crack.

In a large skillet heat oil over medium heat. Add sweet peppers and onion; cook 3 minutes or until softened. Add turkey to skillet; sprinkle with Cajun Seasoning. Cook 4 to 6 minutes or until turkey is no longer pink.

Top coconut wraps with spinach and turkey mixture. Drizzle with Paleo Aïoli; roll up.

>> THANKSGIVING TURKEY STEW <<

MAKES **4** SERVINGS

2 tablespoons extra virgin olive oil

1½ pounds turkey tenderloin, cut into 1-inch cubes

2 cups white mushrooms, quartered

1 cup diced onion

¾ cup diced celery

¾ cup diced parsnips

¼ cup snipped fresh sage or 1 tablespoon dried sage leaves, crushed

1 teaspoon poultry seasoning

⅓ cup dry sherry

4 cups unsalted chicken stock

1 10-ounce package frozen cubed butternut squash or sweet potatoes

1 cup cubed, peeled tart-sweet apple (such as Pink Lady)

3 tablespoons unsalted chicken stock or water

1 tablespoon arrowroot

½ cup fresh or frozen cranberries, thawed if frozen

¼ cup snipped fresh parsley

1 to 2 tablespoons fresh lemon juice

This stew has all the flavors of a Thanksgiving feast in a single pot. You can substitute 3 cups diced cooked turkey for the tenderloins if you like. Don't brown the cooked turkey—just add it to the pot with the stock, squash, and apple as directed.

In a large saucepan heat oil over medium-high heat. Cook half of the turkey in hot oil just until it starts to color (turkey might not be cooked through); remove turkey to bowl. Repeat with remaining turkey, adding more oil if needed. Transfer all turkey to the bowl.

Add mushrooms, onion, celery, parsnips, sage, and poultry seasoning to drippings in pan. Cook and stir 10 minutes or just until vegetables are softened and beginning to brown. Add sherry, stirring to scrape up browned bits from bottom of pan. Simmer, uncovered, until sherry is nearly evaporated. Return turkey to the pan. Add the 4 cups stock, the squash, and apple. Bring to boiling; reduce heat. Cover and simmer 5 minutes or until squash is tender. In a small bowl whisk together the 3 tablespoons stock and the arrowroot until smooth; whisk into stew. Simmer, uncovered, until slightly thickened. Stir in cranberries, parsley, and lemon juice.

TURKEY BURGERS WITH
APPLE-BEET SLAW

>> <<

MAKES **4** SERVINGS

1 to 1¼ pounds uncooked
   ground turkey

4 cloves garlic, minced

1 tablespoon snipped fresh
   tarragon

1 teaspoon paprika

½ teaspoon black pepper

½ teaspoon caraway seeds

¼ cup cider vinegar

¼ cup extra virgin olive oil

1 teaspoon Dijon-Style Mustard
   (recipe, page 304)

3 medium red, yellow, and/or
   orange beets, trimmed, peeled,
   and coarsely shredded

2 medium apples, cored and cut
   into matchstick-size pieces

⅓ cup thinly sliced scallions

¼ cup chopped walnuts, toasted
   (tip, page 63)

Use a food processor to quickly shred the beets and minimize the staining on your hands. Keep in mind that if you use beets of different colors, they will all quickly turn some shade of bright pink if at least one of them is red.

In a large bowl combine turkey, garlic, tarragon, paprika, and pepper. Shape into four ½-inch-thick patties. Grill burgers, uncovered, over medium heat 14 to 18 minutes or until done (165°F), turning once halfway through grilling. (Or grill patties on a stove-top grill pan over medium heat.)

Meanwhile, in a small dry skillet toast caraway seeds over medium heat 1 minute or until very fragrant, shaking skillet occasionally. Let cool. Transfer seeds to a spice grinder; process until finely ground.

For apple-beet slaw, in a large bowl whisk together vinegar, oil, Dijon-Style Mustard, and the ground caraway seeds. Add shredded beets, apples, scallions, and walnuts; toss to coat.

Serve slaw with turkey burgers.

FISH & SHELLFISH

The salt water of the sea and the fresh water of lakes and rivers yield a bounty of protein sources that are light, fresh, and quick-cooking. Salmon, tuna, cod, halibut, sole, trout, shrimp, scallops, crab, and more can be prepared in a variety of ways—pan-seared, grilled, poached, roasted, and stirred into cool, crisp salads.

Broiled Salmon with
Cucumber-Sesame Salsa, *recipe, page 207*

CHOOSING FISH & SHELLFISH

The delicate flesh of fish and shellfish makes them naturally quick-cooking—which makes them ideal for busy weeknight dinners. Most fish is also an excellent source of omega-3-rich protein, so it is a heart-healthy option.

Not all fish offered in the markets is a smart choice, however. Several factors contribute to its healthfulness—both for you as the consumer and for the health of the oceans. The best choice is most often sustainably fished, wild-caught, and—obviously—plentiful. Farm-raised fish have caused concern because the fish are often fed unnatural diets and are crammed into tight enclosures that encourage the spread of disease—which calls for more use of antibiotics. For instance, I do not recommend tilapia at all. However, you also don't want to be eating wild-caught fish that is endangered—or whose populations are shrinking from overfishing. Thankfully, there are a couple of very good resources for smart choices on all fronts. Check out eco-friendly and healthy best choices on the Environmental Defense Fund's website (seafood.edf.org) and the Monterey Bay Aquarium's Seafood Watch (seafoodwatch.org).

COOKING TIMES FOR FISH
FILLETS & STEAKS

BAKE
- In a shallow dish or roasting pan, uncovered, in a 450°F oven for 4 to 6 minutes per ½-inch thickness, until it flakes.

BROIL
- 4 inches from the heat source for 4 to 6 minutes per ½-inch thickness, until it flakes. If fillet is 1 inch or more thick, turn fish once halfway through cooking time.

GRILL
- Over medium heat for 4 to 6 minutes per ½-inch thickness, turning once halfway through cooking time, until it flakes.

PAN-SAUTÉ
- Over medium-high heat 4 to 6 minutes per ½-inch thickness, until it flakes, turning once halfway through cooking time.

POACH
- Bring 1½ cups water, broth, or white wine to boiling in a large skillet. Add fish; return to boiling. Reduce heat and simmer, uncovered, 4 to 6 minutes per ½-inch thickness, until it flakes.

FRESH FISH FACTS

Unless you live on a coast, the fresh fish you buy has probably taken an airplane ride inland from wherever it was pulled from the water. But no matter where you buy your fish—from a coastal fishmonger or a landlocked supermarket, the cues that it is fresh are the same. If it is a whole fish, look for clear, bright, bulging—not sunken—eyes with black pupils. It should have shiny, taught, and bright skin and red gills that are not slippery. The flesh should feel firm and elastic and should be tight to the bone. Fillets and steaks should be cleanly cut and moist. Avoid any fish with a strong "fishy odor," dull or bloody eyes, fading skin with bruises or red spots, or browning or yellowing edges of flesh. Fresh fish is really best cooked the day you buy it. If that's not possible, wrap it loosely in plastic wrap and store it in the coldest spot in your refrigerator—usually the lowest shelf. Cook within 2 days. For longer storage, wrap it tightly in moistureproof/vaporproof wrap and store in the freezer for up to 3 months.

SMOKY SEARED SALMON WITH POMEGRANATE-PARSLEY RELISH

>> <<

4 6-ounce skinless salmon fillets

2 teaspoons Smoky Seasoning
   (recipe, page 296)

4 tablespoons extra virgin olive oil

1 5- to 6-ounce package
   pomegranate seeds

1 cup coarsely chopped fresh
   parsley

1 cup packaged shredded fresh
   carrots

1 shallot, halved and thinly sliced

¼ cup fresh orange juice

2 tablespoons red wine vinegar

½ teaspoon freshly cracked
   black pepper

Searing the salmon at high heat gives it a beautiful crust on the outside. A quick turn in the oven finishes it off so it remains moist and buttery-textured inside. Buying the pomegranate seeds, or arils, already taken out of the fruit saves time and mess.

Preheat oven to 400°F. Rinse fish; pat dry with paper towels. Sprinkle salmon with Smoky Seasoning; rub into fish with your fingers.

In a large oven-safe skillet heat 1 tablespoon of the oil over medium-high heat. Add salmon to skillet; cook about 5 minutes or until lightly browned on both sides, turning once halfway through cooking. Transfer skillet to the preheated oven. Roast about 10 minutes or until salmon flakes easily with a fork.

Meanwhile, for relish, in a medium bowl combine pomegranate seeds, parsley, carrots, shallot, orange juice, vinegar, pepper, and the remaining 3 tablespoons olive oil; toss to coat. Serve with salmon.

SEARED SALMON WITH
>> SUMMER SQUASH, TOMATOES, AND <<
ARUGULA PESTO

MAKES **4** SERVINGS

4 skinless salmon fillets (about
   1½ pounds total)

2 tablespoons extra virgin olive oil
   Freshly ground black pepper

1 tablespoon minced garlic

2 cups diced zucchini

2 cups diced yellow summer squash

1 cup grape tomatoes, halved

⅓ cup Arugula Pesto (recipe,
   page 301)
   Black pepper
   Finely snipped fresh basil
   Lemon wedges

With the pesto ready and waiting in the refrigerator, this brightly colored dish of fish and vegetables can be on the table in 20 to 25 minutes. Dice the summer squash and tomatoes while the salmon is cooking.

Rinse fish; pat dry with paper towels. In a large skillet heat 1 tablespoon of the oil over medium-high heat. Add the salmon fillets, skinned side up; sprinkle with pepper. Cook about 10 minutes or until golden brown and fish flakes easily with a fork, turning once halfway through cooking. Remove salmon and tent with foil to keep warm.

In the same skillet cook the remaining 1 tablespoon oil and the garlic over medium heat until fragrant, about 30 seconds. Add the zucchini and yellow squash. Cook over high heat 3 minutes or until squash begins to brown slightly but is still crisp-tender, stirring occasionally. Stir in the tomatoes; sear 1 to 2 minutes or just until they begin to break down. Remove skillet from heat. Add Arugula Pesto to vegetables; toss gently to coat.

Divide vegetables among four serving plates; top with salmon fillets. Sprinkle with pepper and basil. Serve with lemon wedges.

BROILED SALMON WITH CUCUMBER-SESAME SALSA

>>   <<

MAKES **4** SERVINGS

4 6-ounce salmon fillets

3 tablespoons extra virgin olive oil

2 teaspoons salt-free Chinese five-spice powder

¼ teaspoon black pepper

1 tablespoon white wine vinegar

½ of a large English cucumber, chopped

¼ cup sliced scallions

¼ cup chopped fresh cilantro

2 cloves garlic, minced

2 teaspoons sesame seeds, toasted (tip, page 69)

¼ teaspoon crushed red pepper

Sesame seeds—especially when toasted—add a delightfully nutty flavor to foods. Toast them in a skillet over medium-low heat, stirring frequently, until golden brown. Let them cool completely, then pulse until coarsely ground in a spice blender. Sprinkle over vegetables, meats, poultry, and fish. Store the seasoning in a tightly sealed container in a cool, dark place.

Preheat broiler. Oil the rack of a broiler pan (do not preheat broiler pan). Rinse salmon; pat dry with paper towels. Place salmon on the broiler pan rack. Brush with 1 tablespoon of the oil; sprinkle with five-spice powder and black pepper. Broil 4 inches from the heat until salmon flakes easily when tested with a fork. Allow 4 to 6 minutes per ½-inch thickness of salmon.

Meanwhile, for salsa, in a medium bowl whisk together the remaining 2 tablespoons oil and the vinegar. Add cucumber, scallions, cilantro, garlic, sesame seeds, and crushed red pepper; stir well. Serve fish topped with salsa.

SALMON CAKES WITH
>> LEMONGRASS GREMOLATA <<

MAKES **4** SERVINGS

1 egg, lightly beaten
⅓ cup almond meal
2 tablespoons chopped fresh chives
1 teaspoon fennel seeds, crushed
1 teaspoon ground coriander
3 7.5-ounce cans no-salt-added
   salmon, drained and flaked
   (skin removed and, if desired,
   bones removed)
2 tablespoons coconut oil
2 cups cherry tomatoes
¼ cup chopped onion
1 tablespoon extra virgin olive oil
1 teaspoon snipped fresh rosemary
½ teaspoon black pepper
¼ cup toasted unsalted pistachio
   nuts, chopped
2 tablespoons snipped fresh parsley
1 tablespoon finely chopped
   lemongrass or 1 teaspoon
   lemon zest
1 tablespoon fresh lemon juice
2 cloves garlic, minced

Canned salmon is especially high in calcium if you eat the bones. Fresh salmon bones are too hard to digest, but the canning process softens them and makes them edible. Just crush them into the salmon with a fork.

Preheat oven to 425°F. In a large bowl combine egg, almond meal, chives, fennel seeds, and coriander. Add salmon; mix well. Shape into four ¾-inch-thick patties. In a large skillet heat coconut oil over medium heat. Add salmon patties; cook 8 to 10 minutes or until browned on both sides and heated through (160°F), turning once halfway through cooking.

Meanwhile, in a 2-quart square baking dish combine tomatoes and onion. Drizzle with olive oil; sprinkle with rosemary and ¼ teaspoon of the pepper. Toss to coat. Roast, uncovered, 10 to 12 minutes or just until tomatoes are softened and starting to brown.

For the gremolata, in a small bowl combine pistachio nuts, parsley, lemongrass, lemon juice, garlic, and the remaining ¼ teaspoon pepper.

Top salmon patties with the gremolata; serve with roasted tomatoes and onions.

SEARED TUNA WITH TANGY PEPPER RELISH AND PALEO AÏOLI

>> <<

MAKES **4** SERVINGS

1 medium red sweet pepper

1 medium yellow or orange sweet
   pepper

4 6-ounce skinless tuna steaks,
   cut ¾ to 1 inch thick, or salmon
   fillets

2 teaspoons Mediterranean
   Seasoning (recipe, page 296)

2 tablespoons coconut oil

1 cup thinly sliced celery

¼ cup chopped fresh parsley

¼ cup thinly sliced scallions

2 tablespoons extra virgin olive oil

1 tablespoon white wine vinegar

2 cloves garlic, minced

2 cups torn radicchio

⅓ cup Paleo Aïoli (Garlic Mayo)
   (recipe, page 305)

Tuna is a very lean fish and dries out quickly if overcooked. It should be browned on the outside but still pink—even slightly opaque—in the middle.

Preheat broiler. Cut each sweet pepper into quarters; remove and discard stems, seeds, and membranes. Place peppers, skin sides up, on a foil-lined baking sheet. Broil 5 to 6 inches from the heat 10 to 15 minutes or until skins are evenly charred. Fold corners of foil up around peppers and seal. Let stand 15 minutes or until peppers are cool enough to handle.

Meanwhile, rinse fish; pat dry with paper towels. Sprinkle fish with Mediterranean Seasoning; rub in with your fingers. In a large skillet heat coconut oil over medium-high heat. Add fish; cook 4 to 6 minutes or until fish is browned on the outside and cooked to desired doneness, turning once halfway through cooking. (For salmon, allow 4 to 6 minutes per ½-inch thickness of fish.)

For relish, in a medium bowl combine celery, parsley, scallions, olive oil, vinegar, and garlic. Cut peppers into thin strips; add to relish. Toss to combine.

Thinly slice tuna (if using). Serve fish over radicchio and top with relish and Paleo Aïoli.

>> CAJUN TUNA CAKES ON GREENS <<

1 stalk celery, coarsely chopped

4 scallions, coarsely chopped

1 small red sweet pepper, cored
   and coarsely chopped

5 tablespoons coconut oil

1 avocado, halved, seeded,
   and peeled

1 egg, lightly beaten

¼ cup chopped fresh parsley

2 tablespoons Cajun Seasoning
   (recipe, page 296)

2 tablespoons fresh lemon juice

3 5-ounce cans no-salt-added
   albacore tuna, drained
   and flaked

8 cups mesclun salad mix

1 cup chopped cucumber

1 cup grape tomatoes, halved

⅓ cup Classic French Vinaigrette
   (recipe, page 300)

   Lemon wedges

Crispy on the outside and creamy on the inside—with a pleasing crunch from celery, scallions, and sweet pepper—these tuna cakes make a terrific last-minute meal, especially if you keep cans of no-salt-added tuna in your pantry.

Place celery, scallions, and sweet pepper in a food processor; pulse until diced. In a medium skillet cook celery, scallions, and sweet pepper in 1 tablespoon hot oil 3 minutes or until crisp-tender. Remove skillet from heat; let cool. In a medium bowl mash the avocado. Add egg, parsley, Cajun seasoning, lemon juice, and the cooked vegetables; mix well. Stir in tuna. Shape tuna mixture into eight ¼-inch-thick patties.

In an extra-large skillet heat 2 tablespoons of the oil over medium heat. Cook tuna patties in hot oil for 5 to 6 minutes or until heated through (160°F) and beginning to crisp around the edges, turning once halfway through cooking time. Remove patties from skillet; keep warm while cooking remaining patties in the remaining 2 tablespoons hot oil.

Meanwhile, in a large bowl combine the salad mix, cucumber, and tomatoes; drizzle with Classic French Vinaigrette and toss to coat. Divide salad among four serving plates; add 2 tuna cakes to each plate. Serve with lemon wedges.

SOUTH OF FRANCE-
>> STYLE TUNA SALAD <<

MAKES 4 SERVINGS

6 cups fresh baby spinach

1 8-ounce package steamed and
   peeled baby beets, julienned

8 radishes, trimmed, halved, and
   thinly sliced

2 5- to 6-ounce cans no-salt-added
   tuna, drained and flaked

1 small cucumber, halved and
   thinly sliced

4 Perfectly Steamed Hard-Cooked
   Eggs (recipe, page 256),
   coarsely chopped

2 cups cherry tomatoes, halved
   Small fresh basil leaves

2 tablespoons snipped fresh chives
   Freshly ground black pepper

½ cup Classic French Vinaigrette
   (recipe, page 300)

This fresh and colorful salad was modeled on the classic Niçoise salad—without the non-Paleo ingredients (olives, white potatoes, and green beans). Arrange the ingredients in rows for an especially eye-catching presentation.

Divide spinach among four plates. Arrange beets, radishes, tuna, cucumber, eggs, and tomatoes in rows on top of spinach.

Sprinkle salads with basil, chives, and pepper; drizzle with Classic French Vinaigrette.

GRILLED BLACK PEPPER TUNA AND BABY BOK CHOY WITH CHARRED LIME-GINGER DRIZZLE

>>   <<

MAKES **4** SERVINGS

4   6-ounce tuna steaks, cut 1 inch
    thick

4   tablespoons coconut oil

1   tablespoon freshly ground
    black pepper

½   teaspoon garlic powder

1½ teaspoons Dijon-Style Mustard
    (recipe, page 304)

4   heads baby bok choy, halved
    lengthwise

2   limes, halved crosswise

4   tablespoons walnut oil

2   teaspoon minced fresh ginger

1   clove garlic, minced

Grilled baby bok choy has a fresh, crisp-tender texture and a wonderfully smoky flavor. This simple preparation makes a delicious side dish for grilled meats, fish, and poultry: Just rub with walnut oil (or olive oil), season with black pepper, and grill. Add a squeeze of fresh lime or lemon after it's done, and it's ready to go.

Rinse fish; pat dry with paper towels. In a small bowl combine 2 tablespoons of the coconut oil, the pepper, garlic powder, and 1 teaspoon of the Dijon-Style Mustard; rub onto fish. Drizzle bok choy with the remaining 2 tablespoons coconut oil.

Grill fish, covered, over medium heat for 8 to 10 minutes or until desired doneness, turning once halfway through grilling. Place bok choy and limes, cut sides down, on grill rack; grill 5 minutes or until lightly charred, turning bok choy once. (Or cook tuna, bok choy, and limes on a stove-top grill pan over medium-high heat.)

Squeeze the juice from the grilled limes into a small bowl. Whisk in walnut oil, ginger, garlic, and the remaining ½ teaspoon Dijon-Style Mustard. Drizzle over tuna and bok choy.

FENNEL- AND TOMATO-POACHED
COD FILLETS WITH SPINACH

>>   <<

MAKES **4** SERVINGS

4   6-ounce cod fillets

2   tablespoons extra virgin olive oil

1   fennel bulb, trimmed, cored, halved, and thinly sliced

⅓   cup finely chopped onion

2   cloves garlic, thinly sliced

1   15-ounce can no-salt-added diced tomatoes, drained

2   cups unsalted chicken stock

3   tablespoons vermouth or dry white wine

1   teaspoon snipped fresh thyme

1   teaspoon freshly ground black pepper

1   6-ounce package fresh baby spinach, coarsely chopped

2   tablespoons chopped fresh tarragon or basil

Cod has a mild flavor and a rich, buttery texture that gets even better when it's cooked in a moist environment such as poaching. Serve this dish in shallow bowls with forks and spoons for the delicious poaching liquid made from chicken stock and vermouth infused with tomatoes, thyme, garlic, onion, and fennel.

Rinse fish; pat dry with paper towels.

In a Dutch oven or large skillet heat oil over medium-high heat. Add fennel, onion, and garlic. Cook 5 minutes or just until vegetables are tender. Stir in tomatoes, stock, vermouth, thyme, and ½ teaspoon of the pepper. Bring to boiling.

Sprinkle fish with the remaining ½ teaspoon of the pepper. Nestle fish in the tomato broth so they are about halfway submerged. Cover and simmer 7 minutes. Scatter the chopped spinach around the fish. Cover and cook 3 to 4 minutes more or until the fish flakes easily with a fork.

Using a slotted spoon remove fish, tomatoes, and spinach to shallow bowls. Stir the tarragon into the broth remaining in pot and ladle over the fish.

BROILED COD WITH GREMOLATA
AND CITRUS SALAD

>> <<

MAKES **4** SERVINGS

3 oranges

¼ cup chopped fresh parsley

2 cloves garlic, minced

1 to 1½ pounds cod fillets

3 tablespoons extra virgin olive oil

½ teaspoon black pepper

1 tablespoon white wine vinegar

6 cups fresh baby spinach leaves

¼ cup slivered red onion

Traditional gremolata is a blend of minced parsley, garlic, and lemon zest that is sprinkled over osso buco—the classic Tuscan dish of braised veal shanks—for a pop of color and flavor. There are many contemporary spin-offs of that classic mixture, including this sweeter gremolata featuring orange zest.

Preheat broiler. Lightly oil rack of a broiler pan (do not preheat rack).

Remove 2 teaspoons zest and squeeze 3 tablespoons juice from one orange. Set juice aside. For gremolata, in a bowl stir together the orange zest, the parsley, and garlic.

Rinse fish; pat dry with paper towels. Cut fish into four pieces. Place fish on the prepared rack, tucking under any thin edges. In a small bowl combine the 3 tablespoons orange juice and 1 tablespoon of the oil. Brush fish with juice mixture; sprinkle with pepper. Broil fish 4 inches from the heat until fish flakes easily with a fork (allow 4 to 6 minutes per ½-inch thickness of fish).

Meanwhile, for salad, peel and section the remaining 2 oranges (tip, page 114) over a bowl to catch the juice. Measure 2 tablespoons juice and place in a medium bowl. Whisk in the remaining 2 tablespoons oil and the vinegar. Add orange sections, spinach, and onion. Toss gently to mix.

Top fish with gremolata and serve with salad.

3 WAYS WITH BROCCOLI SLAW MIX

While The Paleo Diet is all about eating fresh, unprocessed foods, there is nothing wrong with taking advantage of some whole foods that are minimally processed (peeled, seeded, shredded, or chopped) and packaged in order to save time in preparing healthful, wholesome meals. Broccoli slaw mix is a perfect example. Made only from shredded broccoli, carrot, and red cabbage, it can be used to make a simple slaw tossed with one of the Paleo salad dressings (page 300) or variations on Paleo Mayo (page 305) and perhaps some additional fruits and vegetables, as with Grilled Salmon with Fruit Slaw (opposite). But broccoli slaw mix can be used in other creative ways as well. In Fish Tacos with Chipotle Mayo (page 220), it's quickly sautéed and seasoned with cilantro and lime juice before being layered into the tacos with cooked fish, avocado, radishes, and a drizzle of spicy mayonnaise. It also serves as the "noodles" in Curried Shrimp and Noodle Bowls (page 221).

GRILLED SALMON
WITH FRUIT SLAW

>> <<

MAKES 4 SERVINGS

4   6-ounce salmon fillets, about
    1 inch thick

2   tablespoons extra virgin olive oil

1   tablespoon Smoky Seasoning
    (recipe, page 296)

1   12-ounce package shredded
    broccoli slaw

1   cup chopped fresh mango

1   medium red sweet pepper,
    seeded and cut into thin bite-
    size strips

¾   cup Bright Citrus Vinaigrette
    (recipe, page 300)

The smoky flavor of the salmon is balanced by the crunchy vinaigrette-dressed slaw sweetened with chunks of fresh, ripe mango.

Rinse fish; pat dry with paper towels. Brush both sides of fish with olive oil; sprinkle with Smoky Seasoning.

Grill fish, covered, over medium heat 8 to 12 minutes or until fish flakes easily with a fork, turning once halfway through grilling. (Or cook fish on a stove-top grill pan over medium heat.)

Meanwhile, for fruit slaw, in a large bowl combine broccoli slaw, mango, and sweet pepper. Drizzle with Bright Citrus Vinaigrette; toss to coat.

Serve grilled salmon with fruit slaw.

FISH TACOS WITH
>> CHIPOTLE MAYO <<

MAKES **4** SERVINGS

1½ pounds halibut fillets

1 tablespoon Mexican Seasoning
(recipe, page 296)

3 tablespoons extra virgin olive oil

1½ cups packaged shredded
broccoli slaw

¼ cup chopped fresh cilantro

1 tablespoon fresh lime juice

8 to 12 large butterhead or Bibb
lettuce leaves

1 avocado, halved, seeded, peeled,
and cut into chunks

¼ cup thinly sliced fresh radishes

½ cup Chipotle Paleo Mayo (recipe,
page 305)

Lime wedges

Halibut is a lean, mild-tasting fish that breaks easily into large chunks or flakes when cooked, making it the perfect fish for filling tacos. Its mildly sweet taste pairs perfectly with the bit of heat from the Mexican Seasoning and Chipotle Mayo.

Rinse fish; pat dry with paper towels. Cut fish into 1-inch chunks. Sprinkle fish with Mexican Seasoning.

In a large skillet heat 2 tablespoons of the oil over medium heat. Add fish to skillet in a single layer; cook 4 to 6 minutes or until fish flakes easily with a fork, turning once halfway through cooking. Remove fish; cover to keep warm.

Wipe out skillet with paper towels. Heat the remaining 1 tablespoon oil in skillet over medium heat. Add broccoli slaw; cook and stir 3 to 4 minutes or until crisp-tender. Remove skillet from heat; stir in cilantro and lime juice.

Fill lettuce leaves with cooked slaw, fish, avocado, and radishes. Drizzle tacos with Chipotle Paleo Mayo. Serve with lime wedges.

>> CURRIED SHRIMP NOODLE BOWLS <<

MAKES 4 SERVINGS

- 2 tablespoons coconut oil
- 1 large red or yellow sweet pepper, seeded and cut into bite-size strips
- ½ cup thinly sliced onion
- 1 8-ounce package sliced fresh cremini mushrooms
- 1 tablespoon minced fresh ginger
- 4 cloves garlic, minced
- 1 12-ounce package shredded broccoli slaw
- 1 13.5-ounce can unsweetened coconut milk
- 4 teaspoons salt-free Thai red curry powder
- 1 pound cooked and peeled large shrimp (thawed if frozen)
- ½ cup fresh cilantro leaves
- 2 tablespoons fresh lime juice
  Lime wedges

Most prepared Thai curry pastes and powders contain salt—and some contain sugar. A highly flavorful salt- and sugar-free Thai red curry powder is available online from The Spice House at thespicehouse.com.

In an extra-large skillet heat coconut oil over medium-high heat. Add sweet pepper and onion; cook and stir 2 minutes. Add mushrooms; cook and stir 3 minutes or until vegetables are crisp-tender. Add ginger and garlic; cook and stir 1 minute or until fragrant. Add broccoli slaw; cook 2 minutes. Stir in coconut milk and curry powder. Bring to boiling; reduce heat. Simmer, uncovered, 2 minutes or until slightly reduced. Add shrimp; simmer until shrimp are heated through. Stir in ¼ cup of the cilantro and the lime juice.

Divide among four serving bowls. Top with the remaining ¼ cup cilantro and serve with lime wedges.

BROILED HALIBUT WITH ASPARAGUS-HERB SALAD

>>   <<

MAKES **4** SERVINGS

4   6-ounce halibut steaks, cut 1 inch thick

½   cup Classic French Vinaigrette (recipe, page 300)

     Extra virgin olive oil

1   pound thick asparagus spears

¼   cup chopped fresh parsley

2   tablespoons chopped fresh chives

2   teaspoons lemon zest

When making an asparagus ribbon salad, it's best to have thicker spears to yield more ribbons per stalk. It's also easier to shave the ribbons from a thicker stalk.

Rinse fish; pat dry with paper towels. Place fish in a shallow glass dish. For marinade, pour ¼ cup of Classic French Vinaigrette over the fish, turning fish to coat both sides. Let stand 5 minutes.

Preheat broiler. Remove fish from marinade; discard marinade. Brush the rack of a broiler pan with oil; place fish on the rack. Broil fish 4 inches from the heat 7 to 9 minutes or until fish flakes easily with a fork

Meanwhile, for asparagus-herb salad, snap off and discard woody bases from asparagus. Using a vegetable peeler, shave asparagus spears into long thin ribbons. In a medium bowl combine shaved asparagus, parsley, chives, and lemon zest. Drizzle with the remaining ¼ cup Classic French Vinaigrette; toss to coat.

Serve fish with asparagus-herb salad.

>> GINGER-COCONUT FISH SOUP <<

MAKES **4** SERVINGS

1 cup frozen mirepoix blend
   vegetables (chopped onion,
   celery, and carrots)

1 tablespoon coconut oil

2 tablespoons finely chopped
   fresh ginger

4 cloves garlic, minced

4 cups unsalted vegetable stock

2 large sweet potatoes (about
   12 ounces), peeled and cubed

¼ teaspoon crushed red pepper
   (optional)

1 pound skinless halibut fillets

1 tablespoon salt-free Chinese
   five-spice powder

1 medium zucchini, cut into thin
   bite-size strips

1 cup unsweetened coconut milk*

½ cup fresh basil leaves, cut into thin
   ribbons

¼ cup unsweetened shredded
   coconut, lightly toasted (tip,
   page 159)

If you haven't tried fish soup before, then this is the recipe to try. The fish cooks quickly in a savory broth and is finished with rich coconut milk.

In a 4-quart Dutch oven cook mirepoix vegetables in hot coconut oil over medium heat 5 minutes, stirring occasionally. Add ginger and garlic; cook and stir 1 minute. Add stock, sweet potatoes, and, if desired, crushed red pepper. Bring to boiling; reduce heat. Cover and simmer 10 minutes.

Meanwhile, rinse fish; pat dry with paper towels. Cut fish into 1-inch pieces. In a medium bowl gently toss fish cubes with five-spice powder. Add fish and zucchini to soup. Return to boiling; reduce heat. Cover and simmer 3 to 5 minutes or until fish flakes easily when tested with a fork and vegetables are tender. Stir in coconut milk. Cook 1 minute over low heat. Sprinkle servings with basil and coconut.

*Tip: Thoroughly mix the coconut milk before measuring to incorporate the coconut cream that rises to the top with the rest of the liquid.

>> PECAN-CRUSTED RED SNAPPER <<

MAKES **4** SERVINGS

4 6- to 8-ounce red snapper fillets

¾ cup chopped pecans

1 tablespoon extra virgin olive oil

1 tablespoon lemon zest

3 cloves garlic, minced

2 tablespoons snipped fresh parsley

¼ teaspoon black pepper

⅛ to ¼ teaspoon cayenne pepper

   Lemon wedges

Serve this simple fish with oven-roasted sweet potato wedges. Toss ½-inch wedges of peeled sweet potatoes with olive oil, crushed red pepper, onion powder, and garlic powder. Arrange in a single layer on a rimmed baking sheet and bake at 400°F for 30 minutes. Add the fish to the oven after the potatoes have been in about 15 minutes.

Preheat oven to 400°F. Rinse fish; pat dry with paper towels. In a small bowl combine pecans, olive oil, lemon zest, garlic, parsley, black pepper, and cayenne pepper.

Place fish fillets, skin sides down, on a rimmed baking sheet. Spoon pecan mixture over fillets, spreading slightly; press lightly to help it adhere to fish.

Bake 12 to 15 minutes or until fish flakes easily with a fork. Serve with lemon wedges.

POACHED SOLE WITH
>> LEMONGRASS, GINGER, <<
AND GREEN TEA

MAKES **4** SERVINGS

1¼ cups water

1 or 2 green tea bags

½ cup dry white wine

1 tablespoon thinly sliced lemongrass (about 1 stalk)

1 teaspoon grated fresh ginger

¼ teaspoon ground turmeric

1 pound asparagus spears

1 pound sole or orange roughy fillets, about ½ inch thick

1 tablespoon arrowroot

1 tablespoon fresh lemon juice

Snipped fresh chives

Freshly ground black pepper

Turmeric root is more widely available today than it has been in the past and can be substituted here for a fresher flavor. If desired, use 1 teaspoon grated fresh turmeric in place of the ground dried turmeric.

In a large skillet bring 1 cup of the water to boiling; reduce heat. Add tea bag(s); cover and let steep 3 minutes. Discard tea bag(s). Stir in wine, lemongrass, ginger, and turmeric.

Carefully add the asparagus, halving stalks if needed to fit in skillet. Arrange fish on top of asparagus. Cook, covered, over medium-low heat 6 minutes or until fish flakes easily with a fork and asparagus is crisp-tender. With a slotted spatula, remove asparagus and fish to a platter; cover and keep warm.

For sauce, in a small bowl whisk together the remaining ¼ cup water and the arrowroot until smooth; whisk into cooking liquid in skillet. Cook and stir 1 minute or until thickened and bubbly. Stir in lemon juice. Spoon sauce over fish and asparagus. Sprinkle with chives and pepper.

Fragrant Braised Halibut Fillets,
recipe, page 222

FRAGRANT BRAISED HALIBUT FILLETS

>>   <<

MAKES 4 SERVINGS

1 tablespoon ground cumin

1 tablespoon freshly ground
   black pepper

2 teaspoons salt-free Aleppo
   pepper flakes or ground ancho
   chile pepper

2 teaspoons paprika

2 teaspoons ground cinnamon

¼ teaspoon ground saffron

3 tablespoons extra virgin olive oil

4 boneless halibut or striped bass
   fillets, 1½ inches thick
   (1 to 1½ pounds total)

1 medium zucchini, chopped

1 small Vidalia onion, halved and
   thinly sliced

4 cloves garlic, minced

1 large beefsteak tomato, cored
   and chopped

¼ cup fresh lemon juice

3 tablespoons minced fresh parsley

Aleppo pepper is grown primarily in Turkey and Syria and is widely used in Middle Eastern cooking. It is moderately hot—similar to an ancho chile—with a touch of sweet, fruity, and cumin undertones. It is often processed with salt, but there are no-salt-added varieties available. If you can't find it, ground ancho chile is a fine substitute.

In a small bowl combine cumin, black pepper, Aleppo pepper, paprika, cinnamon, and saffron. Rub spice mixture evenly over fish fillets.

In a large nonstick skillet heat 2 tablespoons of the olive oil over medium-high heat. Cook fish in the hot oil about 5 minutes or until lightly browned, turning once. Remove fish from skillet.

Add the remaining 1 tablespoon olive oil to the skillet. Stir in zucchini, onion, and garlic. Cook about 5 minutes or just until zucchini and onion begin to soften. Stir in tomato. Bring to boiling. Place fish over the vegetables in the skillet. Cover and cook about 8 minutes or until fish flakes easily with a fork.

Before serving, drizzle with lemon juice and sprinkle with parsley.

LEMON-GARLIC SOLE WITH CURRIED PARSNIP SLAW

>>   <<

MAKES 4 SERVINGS

1¼ to 1½ pounds skinless sole fillets

1 tablespoon lemon zest

1 tablespoon minced garlic
(6 cloves)

1 tablespoon extra virgin olive oil

½ teaspoon freshly ground black
pepper

2 large carrots

2 large parsnips

½ cup thinly sliced scallions

⅓ cup Paleo Mayo (recipe,
page 305)

2 tablespoons rice vinegar

½ teaspoon ground ginger

¼ teaspoon ground turmeric

¼ teaspoon ground coriander

¼ teaspoon ground cumin

⅛ teaspoon ground nutmeg

⅛ teaspoon cayenne pepper

2 tablespoons sesame seeds,
toasted (tip, page 69)

Sole is very thin and bakes quickly. For most fish, a good guideline for baking fish is 4 to 6 minutes per ½-inch thickness at 450°F.

Preheat oven to 450°F. Line a large baking sheet with parchment paper. Rinse fish; pat dry with paper towels. Place fish on prepared baking sheet. In a small bowl combine lemon zest, garlic, oil, and black pepper. Spread evenly on fish; set aside.

For slaw, peel carrots and parsnips. Using a julienne peeler, cut carrots and parsnips into long thin shreds. In a large bowl combine carrots, parsnips, and scallions. For dressing, in a small bowl stir together Paleo Mayo, vinegar, ginger, turmeric, coriander, cumin, nutmeg, and cayenne pepper. Add dressing to vegetables; stir to coat.

Measure thickness of fish. Bake fish 4 to 6 minutes per ½-inch thickness or until fish flakes easily with a fork.

Sprinkle slaw with sesame seeds; toss to combine. Serve fish with slaw.

>> PEPITA-CRUSTED TROUT <<

MAKES **4** SERVINGS

½ cup pepitas (pumpkin seeds)

1 tablespoon Lemon-Herb
   Seasoning (recipe, page 296)

1 egg, lightly beaten

2 tablespoons water

1 pound trout fillets with skin

3 tablespoons coconut oil

2 4.5-ounce packages baby kale

½ cup shredded carrot

1 tablespoon extra virgin olive oil

⅓ cup naturally sweetened,
   unsulfured dried cranberries

3 tablespoons fresh lemon juice
   Lemon wedges

Ground pumpkin seeds mixed with Lemon-Herb Seasoning make a crisp and tasty coating on these trout fillets. A side of kale sautéed with shredded carrots and studded with tart dried cranberries adds color and nutrition to the plate.

In a food processor pulse pepitas to make a coarse flour. Transfer pepita flour to a small bowl; stir in Lemon-Herb Seasoning. In another small bowl whisk together egg and the water.

Rinse fish; pat dry with paper towels. Cut fish into four serving-size pieces. Brush skinless side of each piece with egg wash and top with 2 tablespoons of the pepita mixture; press lightly to help it adhere to fish.

In a large heavy skillet heat coconut oil over medium-high heat. Fry fillets in hot oil, in batches if necessary, 2 to 3 minutes or until bottoms are golden; carefully turn fish and fry 3 minutes more.

Meanwhile, in another large skillet cook kale and carrot in hot olive oil over medium-high heat 1 minute or just until kale begins to wilt. Remove skillet from heat. Add cranberries and lemon juice; toss to combine. Serve fish with kale and lemon wedges.

ARCTIC CHAR WITH
>> CAULIFLOWER COUSCOUS AND <<
TOASTED MACADAMIA DRIZZLE

MAKES 4 SERVINGS

1 small head cauliflower, broken
into large florets

4 tablespoons extra virgin olive oil

2 tablespoons raw pumpkin seeds
(pepitas)

2 teaspoons cumin seeds

2 tablespoons fresh lemon juice

4 6- to 8-ounce arctic char or
salmon fillets with skin

1 recipe Macadamia Nut Dressing
(recipe, page 300)

Snipped fresh parsley (optional)

Lemon wedges (optional)

Arctic char is a coldwater fish that is related to both salmon and trout. It has characteristics of both—the pretty pink color of salmon but the fine texture and more delicate flavor of trout.

In a food processor pulse cauliflower (in batches if necessary) until the pieces are the size of couscous. In a large skillet cook cauliflower couscous in 2 tablespoons of the oil about 5 minutes or until tender and just beginning to brown, stirring occasionally. Remove to a large bowl.

Meanwhile, in another large skillet toast pumpkin and cumin seeds over medium heat 2 minutes or until fragrant and lightly browned, stirring constantly. Add toasted seeds and 1 tablespoon of the lemon juice to the cauliflower couscous. Toss to combine. Cover to keep warm.

Using a sharp knife, make two cuts through the skin on fish fillets but not into the flesh. Grill fish, skin sides down, over medium heat 3 minutes or until skin is crisp. Carefully turn fish; grill 3 minutes more or until fish flakes easily with a fork. (Or grill fish on a stove-top grill pan over medium heat.) Drizzle fish with the remaining 1 tablespoon lemon juice.

Spoon Macadamia Nut Dressing over fish and, if desired, sprinkle with parsley. Serve with cauliflower couscous and, if desired, lemon wedges.

ARCTIC CHAR WITH
>> CRISPY GARLIC-LIME SAUCE <<
AND CUMIN CARROTS

MAKES **4** SERVINGS

5 cloves garlic

1 pound packaged peeled
   baby carrots

4 tablespoons extra virgin olive oil

1½ teaspoons cumin seeds, crushed

4 6-ounce arctic char fillets, about
   1 inch thick

4 tablespoons fresh lime juice

¼ teaspoon black pepper

2 tablespoons finely chopped onion

2 teaspoons snipped fresh cilantro
   (optional)

The time-saving trick in this recipe is to broil the fish in the oven but cook the carrots in the microwave until they're tender—then just give them a quick pass under the broiler to brown them. The process replicates roasting the carrots without taking up the oven space you need for broiling—and dramatically shortens the 30 minutes of roasting time.

Preheat broiler. Thinly slice 3 of the cloves of the garlic and mince the remaining 2 cloves garlic. In a microwave-safe bowl combine carrots, 2 tablespoons of the oil, the minced garlic, and cumin seeds. Cover with vented plastic wrap and microwave 7 to 8 minutes or just until tender, stirring once. Place carrots on a foil-lined baking sheet. Broil 3 to 4 inches from heat 2 to 3 minutes or until lightly browned, turning once. Cover to keep warm.

Rinse fish; pat dry with paper towels. Place fish on the unheated rack of a broiler pan. Brush fish with 1 tablespoon of the lime juice; sprinkle with ⅛ teaspoon of the pepper.

Broil fish 3 to 4 inches from the heat 8 to 10 minutes or until fish flakes easily with a fork.

Meanwhile, for garlic-lime sauce, in a small skillet heat the remaining 2 tablespoons olive oil over medium-high heat. Add the sliced garlic and onion; cook and stir until tender and golden. Stir in remaining 3 tablespoons lime juice and the remaining ⅛ teaspoon pepper. Bring to boiling; remove from heat.

Spoon sauce over fish and, if desired, sprinkle fish with cilantro. Serve with cumin carrots.

>> CAJUN SHRIMP EN PAPILLOTE <<

MAKES **4** SERVINGS

1½ pounds peeled and deveined
   extra-large shrimp

1 tablespoon Cajun Seasoning
   (recipe, page 296)

1 lemon

1 large red sweet pepper, cut into
   ½-inch strips

1 large green sweet pepper, cut
   into ½-inch strips

1 stalk celery, thinly sliced

1 small onion, cut into thin wedges

3 tablespoons extra virgin olive oil

1 medium avocado, halved, seeded,
   peeled, and chopped

1 medium tomato, seeded and
   chopped

1 tablespoon snipped fresh cilantro

1 tablespoon snipped fresh parsley

Cooking "en papillote" is a French method of cooking in packets made of parchment (and sometimes foil). This method helps retain nutrients and flavor in foods, and the steam that builds up during cooking helps retain moisture. This recipe includes a simple method for making your own parchment packets, but if you can find them, parchment cooking bags that make the process even simpler are available.

Preheat oven to 450°F. In a medium bowl combine shrimp and Cajun Seasoning; toss to coat. Using a vegetable peeler, remove the outer peel from the lemon in long strips, making sure not to pick up any of the bitter white pith. Squeeze 1 tablespoon juice from the lemon.

Cut four 20×12-inch pieces of parchment paper. Fold in half to crease parchment and unfold. Divide red and green sweet peppers, celery, onion, and the lemon peel strips among parchment paper sheets, placing the vegetables on one half of a sheet. Drizzle with 2 tablespoons of the oil. Top vegetables with shrimp.

To seal packets, fold parchment along the crease over shrimp. Working in 2-inch sections, fold about ¼ inch of the open edges over and crease tightly; fold again. Continue working around the edge, overlapping folded sections slightly. Finish with a double fold at the end of the packet. Crease folds tightly so they don't open. Place packets on an extra-large baking sheet.

Bake 10 to 12 minutes or until shrimp are opaque. Meanwhile, for avocado salsa, in a small bowl combine avocado, tomato, cilantro, parsley, and the remaining 1 tablespoon oil; toss gently to combine.

To serve, cut an "X" in tops of parchment packets. Spoon salsa into packets.

>> MANGO SHRIMP SALAD <<

MAKES **4** SERVINGS

1 mango

½ cup chilled Paleo Mayo (recipe, page 305)

1 to 2 tablespoons balsamic vinegar

1 teaspoon finely grated fresh ginger

1 teaspoon salt-free curry powder

12 ounces cooked, peeled, and deveined shrimp, coarsely chopped

¼ cup chopped celery

2 tablespoons chopped red onion

8 large butter lettuce leaves

2 to 3 tablespoons shredded radishes (optional)

If you buy frozen cooked shrimp, be sure to read the label to ensure that the only ingredient listed is "shrimp"—no preservatives or salt.

Halve the mango, cutting on each side of the seed. Cut the fruit in each half into thin slices; remove from skin and set aside. Cut any remaining mango from around the seed and finely chop.

In a large bowl stir together the finely chopped mango, Paleo Mayo, balsamic vinegar, ginger, and curry powder. Stir in shrimp, celery, and onion.

Divide lettuce among plates and top with mango slices. Spoon shrimp mixture on mango slices. If desired, top with radishes.

CITUS SHRIMP SALAD
>> WITH TOMATOES, ORANGES, << AND FENNEL

- 1 Meyer lemon or other lemon
- 2 oranges (navel, Cara Cara, and/or blood oranges, and/or tangerines)
- 3 tablespoons white wine vinegar
- 1 small shallot, minced
- ¼ cup extra virgin olive oil
- 1 tablespoon finely snipped fresh tarragon
- 1 tablespoon finely snipped fresh chives
-   Black pepper
- 1½ pounds cooked, peeled, and deveined large shrimp
- 1 small fennel bulb, trimmed, cored, and shaved
- 1 cup grape tomatoes, halved
- ¼ cup thinly sliced red onion
- 8 cups mesclun salad greens

If the leafy fronds of the fennel stalks look fresh and healthy, chop a few and use as a garnish and flavor boost on top of this summery salad.

Remove 2 teaspoons zest and squeeze 3 tablespoons juice from the lemon. Place lemon juice in a large bowl. Remove 2 tablespoons zest from oranges. Section oranges (tip, page 114). After removing orange sections, squeeze the membranes to extract the juice into the bowl with the lemon juice.

For vinaigrette, add vinegar and shallot to the citrus juice. Slowly drizzle in the olive oil, whisking until emulsified. Add the tarragon, chives, and pepper to taste.

Add the shrimp to the vinaigrette; toss to coat. Let stand 10 minutes.

To serve, add the shaved fennel, tomatoes, and onion to the shrimp and toss gently to mix. Divide mesclun among four serving plates; top with shrimp and vegetables. If desired, drizzle with vinaigrette remaining in the bowl.

GAZPACHO WITH SHRIMP
AND AVOCADO RELISH

>>   <<

MAKES 4 SERVINGS

1 pound roma tomatoes, seeded
   and coarsely chopped

1 medium cucumber, peeled and
   coarsely chopped

¾ cup chopped red sweet pepper

¼ cup chopped fresh cilantro

3 tablespoons chopped red onion

2 tablespoons fresh lemon juice

1 tablespoon minced, seeded
   jalapeño chile (tip, page 37)

1 clove garlic

¾ cup no-salt-added tomato juice

1 pound peeled, deveined, and
   cooked shrimp, coarsely
   chopped

1 recipe Avocado Relish

This is a cool and refreshing meal for a hot summer night, when you don't want to cook on the stove, turn on the oven—or even light the grill outside.

In a blender or food processor combine tomatoes, cucumber, sweet pepper, cilantro, red onion, lemon juice, jalapeño, garlic, and tomato juice. Cover and pulse until smooth. Transfer soup to a large bowl; stir in shrimp.

Serve soup with Avocado Relish.

Avocado Relish: In a medium bowl combine 1 ripe avocado, peeled, seeded, and diced; ¼ cup finely chopped red sweet pepper; 2 tablespoons snipped fresh cilantro; 1 tablespoon finely chopped red onion; and 1 tablespoon fresh lemon juice.

PARSNIP NOODLES WITH LUMP CRAB AND CHERMOULA

>>   <<

5 tablespoons extra virgin olive oil

2 large red sweet peppers, cored, seeded, and chopped

1 cup chopped yellow onion

1 pound parsnips, cut into noodles*

2 cups packed fresh cilantro leaves

1½ cups packed fresh parsley leaves

4 cloves garlic

2 teaspoons sweet paprika

2 teaspoons cumin seeds, lightly toasted (tip, page 63)

½ teaspoon coriander seeds, lightly toasted (tip, page 63)

¼ teaspoon cayenne pepper

⅛ teaspoon crushed saffron (optional)

¼ cup fresh lemon juice

½ cup extra virgin olive oil

2 cups cooked lump crabmeat, coarsely flaked (headnote, page 249)

Chopped fresh parsley and cilantro (optional)

Born in Morocco, chermoula is a rich blend of spices and herbs with a hint of floral (that's the coriander), but there's not one specific recipe for it. Cooks in different regions add their own spins on the blend. It is traditionally served with grilled fish, but its use has spread to vegetables, beef, and chicken.

In an extra-large skillet heat 2 tablespoons olive oil over medium heat. Add sweet peppers and onion; cook 3 to 4 minutes or until crisp-tender. Remove from skillet; keep warm. Add 3 tablespoons olive oil to the skillet and return to medium heat. Add parsnip noodles. Cover and cook 5 to 7 minutes or until crisp-tender, stirring occasionally. Remove skillet from heat. Add sweet peppers and onions to parsnips in skillet; toss to combine.

Meanwhile, for chermoula, in a food processor or blender combine 2 cups cilantro, 1½ cups parsley, the garlic, paprika, cumin seeds, coriander seeds, cayenne, and, if desired, saffron. Pulse until coarsely chopped. Add lemon juice and pulse until combined. With the processor running, slowly add olive oil in a thin, steady stream (chermoula thickens as oil is added).

Add ½ cup of the chermoula to the vegetables; toss to coat. (Reserve remaining chermoula for another use.**) Add crabmeat to vegetables and gently toss. If desired, sprinkle with additional chopped parsley and cilantro.

*Tip: To cut parsnips into noodles, trim off ends. Use a vegetable spiralizer, julienne cutter, or mandoline to cut parsnips into long, thin noodles.

**Tip: The recipe makes 1½ cups chermoula. Store the leftover chermoula in a tightly covered container in the refrigerator up to 1 week. Or divide into smaller portions and freeze up to 3 months.

ZUCCHINI PANCAKES WITH
CHARRED JALAPEÑO SHRIMP SALAD

>> <<

MAKES **4** SERVINGS

2 or 3 jalapeño chiles, halved
   lengthwise and seeded (tip,
   page 37)

⅓ cup Macadamia Nut Dressing
   (recipe, page 300)

1 teaspoon paprika

1 teaspoon lemon zest

½ teaspoon black pepper

½ teaspoon celery seeds

¼ teaspoon onion powder

1 pound cooked, peeled, and
   deveined shrimp, coarsely
   chopped

2 medium zucchini

2 eggs

½ cup almond flour

1 teaspoon Lemon-Herb Seasoning
   (recipe, page 296)

2 tablespoons chopped fresh
   parsley

1 clove garlic, minced

¼ to ½ cup extra virgin olive oil

For speed, shred the zucchini in a food processor fitted with the shredding blade, if you have one. Keep the cooked zucchini pancakes warm on a paper towel-lined rimmed baking sheet in a 200°F oven while you cook the remaining batter.

Preheat broiler. Place jalapeños, skin sides up, on a broiler pan. Broil about 3 inches from heat 5 minutes or until charred. Let peppers cool until easy to handle. Finely chop cooled jalapeños.

Meanwhile, for salad, in a medium bowl combine Macadamia Nut Dressing, paprika, lemon zest, black pepper, celery seeds, and onion powder. Stir in shrimp and charred jalapeños. Chill until needed.

For pancakes, coarsely shred zucchini. Place shredded zucchini in a clean kitchen towel and squeeze out excess moisture. In a medium bowl whisk together eggs, almond flour, Lemon-Herb Seasoning, parsley, and garlic. Stir in zucchini. Heat a large skillet over medium-high heat. Add enough olive oil to coat the bottom of the skillet. Working in batches, spoon about ¼ cup of the batter into the skillet for each pancake, spreading into ¼-inch-thick patties. Cook 1 to 2 minutes per side or until golden brown. Add more oil as needed.

>> SEARED SEA SCALLOPS <<

2   pounds large sea scallops

¼   teaspoon black pepper

2   tablespoons extra virgin olive oil

2   cups chopped fresh tomatoes

⅓   cup Roasted Garlic Vinaigrette
    (recipe, page 300)

¼   cup chopped fresh parsley

2   teaspoons lemon zest

Get the scallops as dry as possible before searing them in the skillet. The drier they are, the better they will take on a beautiful exterior crust.

_____

Rinse scallops; pat dry with paper towels. Sprinkle scallops with pepper.

In a large skillet heat the oil over medium-high heat. Add scallops; cook 4 to 5 minutes or until browned and opaque, turning once halfway through cooking.

Meanwhile, in a large bowl combine tomatoes, Roasted Garlic Vinaigrette, parsley, and lemon zest. Serve with scallops.

CHAMPAGNE-POACHED
>> SCALLOP SALAD <<

MAKES **4** SERVINGS

16 large sea scallops (1 pound)
 1 large fennel bulb
 2 cups champagne or dry white
     wine, such as Chardonnay
     (not oaky)
 2 fresh thyme sprigs
 2 fresh dill sprigs
 1 tablespoon fresh lemon juice
     Freshly ground black pepper
 ¼ cup extra virgin olive oil
 1 10-ounce package herb blend
     salad
 2 tablespoons snipped fresh chives

If you opt to use Chardonnay to poach the scallops instead of champagne, look for one with fruity, rather than oaky, flavor—or even an unoaked Chardonnay. If the wine has a strong oak flavor, it will overpower the delicate flavor of the scallops.

Rinse scallops; pat dry with paper towels. Remove fronds from fennel and set aside. Cut fennel bulb into quarters; cut out and discard core. Slice fennel bulb.

In a large saucepan combine fennel slices and fronds, champagne, thyme, and dill. Bring to boiling; add scallops. Return to boiling; reduce heat. Simmer about 6 minutes or until scallops are opaque. Remove scallops to a baking sheet. Strain poaching liquid; measure ¼ cup strained liquid (discard remaining liquid). Place baking sheet and the poaching liquid in the freezer for 10 minutes or until thoroughly chilled.

For dressing, in a small bowl combine chilled liquid, lemon juice, and pepper to taste. Gradually whisk in olive oil until emulsified.

Place herb blend salad in a large bowl and drizzle with half of the dressing. Toss scallops with the remaining dressing. Divide herb blend among four plates. Top with scallops; sprinkle with chives and additional pepper.

GRILLED SCALLOPS WITH ASPARAGUS AND PEPPERS

>> <<

MAKES **4** SERVINGS

16 large sea scallops (about 1 pound)
1 tablespoon ground allspice
1 teaspoon hot Hungarian paprika
½ teaspoon freshly ground black pepper
1½ pounds thin asparagus spears
2 tablespoons extra virgin olive oil
1 yellow sweet pepper, seeded and cut into strips
2 tablespoons fresh lemon juice
¼ cup fresh chopped parsley (optional)

Most Hungarian paprika sold in this country is the sweet or mild variety. This recipe calls for the hot stuff. If you don't like your food spicy, sweet paprika will provide the pretty red color you see here—but no heat.

Rinse scallops; pat dry with paper towels. In a small bowl stir together allspice, paprika, and black pepper. Sprinkle the spice mixture on both sides of scallops.

Snap off tough ends from asparagus. Drizzle asparagus and sweet pepper strips with the olive oil. Toss to coat.

Heat a stove-top grill pan over medium-high heat. Cook vegetables, half at a time, 6 to 8 minutes or until crisp-tender and grill marks appear, turning once halfway through cooking. Remove vegetables; cover with foil to keep warm.

Brush the grill pan with additional olive oil. Cook the scallops, in batches if necessary, over medium-high heat about 6 minutes or until opaque, turning once halfway through cooking.

Serve grilled scallops over vegetables. Drizzle with the lemon juice and, if desired, sprinkle with parsley.

Tip: If you prefer, cook scallops, asparagus, and sweet pepper on an outdoor grill. Be sure to place asparagus and pepper strips perpendicular to grates on the grill and use a grill basket for the scallops.

>> CRUNCHY CRAB SALAD <<

MAKES 4 TO 6 SERVINGS

½ teaspoon cumin seeds

1½ cups cooked crabmeat
(12 ounces), coarsely flaked

1 medium avocado, halved, seeded,
peeled, and chopped

⅔ cup coarsely shredded English
cucumber

½ cup very thinly sliced radishes

½ cup thinly sliced celery

¼ cup thinly sliced scallions

¼ cup snipped fresh cilantro

2 limes

2 tablespoons avocado oil or
olive oil

⅛ to ¼ teaspoon crushed red pepper

8 to 12 butterhead lettuce leaves

Toasted cumin seeds (optional)

Crushed red pepper (optional)

Unless you live on a coast, good-quality cooked crabmeat may be difficult to find. Even if it has no added salt, canned crabmeat varies wildly in quality. Look for refrigerated packages of cooked crabmeat—with no added salt or preservatives—as the second-best option to buying in bulk from a fishmonger.

In a small dry skillet heat cumin seeds over medium heat 1 to 2 minutes or until fragrant, shaking skillet occasionally. Transfer seeds to a mortar and pestle or spice grinder; coarsely grind seeds.

In a large bowl combine crabmeat, avocado, cucumber, radishes, celery, scallions, and cilantro.

For dressing, remove 1 teaspoon zest and squeeze 3 tablespoons juice from limes. In a small bowl whisk together the ground cumin seeds, lime zest and juice, oil, and crushed red pepper. Drizzle over crab salad; toss gently to coat.

Spoon crab salad onto lettuce leaves. If desired, sprinkle with additional toasted cumin seeds and crushed red pepper.

>> CRAB-STUFFED AVOCADOS <<

MAKES **4** SERVINGS

1½ cups cooked crabmeat
   (12 ounces), coarsely flaked
   (see headnote, page 249)

½ cup finely chopped red sweet
   pepper

⅓ cup Paleo Mayo (recipe,
   page 305)

¼ cup snipped fresh parsley

¼ cup thinly sliced scallions

4 ripe avocados, halved lengthwise
   and seeded

1 cup fresh broccoli, sunflower, or
   radish microgreens

Lemon wedges (optional)

To get the best-quality avocados, buy them when they are bright green and quite firm, then leave at room temperature for a couple days to ripen—until they yield just slightly when pressed lightly with your thumb. If they are firm when brought home from the store, they are less likely to get bruised and blemished.

For filling, in a medium bowl stir together crabmeat, sweet pepper, Paleo Mayo, parsley, and scallions.

Divide filling among avocado halves. Sprinkle with microgreens and serve with lemon wedges.

Portobellos with Poached
Eggs and Sweet Pepper
Sauté, recipe, page 277

EGGS & SMOOTHIES

With just a few simple ingredients—eggs, nut milks, fruits, vegetables, and herbs—you can make a quick, satisfying, and healthful meal in minutes. Eggs are a staple and a terrific source of protein—and they're incredibly versatile. These egg and smoothie recipes are suitable for any time of day—breakfast, lunch, or a super quick supper.

GOOD EGGS

The proliferation of urban chicken coops in recent years is a good indication of the value of good, fresh eggs. If you don't happen to have a backyard coop—or don't know someone who does—you have to buy your eggs. There is a lot of confusing labeling around eggs. Farm-fresh or pastured eggs are the best choice for both quality and animal health. Pastured eggs are produced by chickens that roam freely and forage for their natural diet of seeds and insects. Find them at farmers markets, co-ops, natural-food stores, and from the producer. If you can't, make the best choice at the supermarket:

CERTIFIED ORGANIC: In a typical scenario, thousands of birds are very tightly packed but uncaged in warehouses. They have some outdoor access, but there are no USDA rules governing size of the space, time allowed, or quality of it. They are fed an all-vegetarian diet free of antibiotics and pesticides.

NATURAL: The USDA stipulates only that the eggs have no artificial ingredients or added color and are minimally processed. Because this applies to most eggs, the term really lacks any meaning.

CAGE-FREE: The hens are uncaged and very tightly packed inside warehouses but generally don't have access outside. There are no restrictions on diet.

FREE-RANGE: The hens are uncaged and very tightly packed in warehouses. They have some outdoor access, but there are no USDA rules governing size of the space, time allowed, or quality of it. There are no restrictions on diet.

THE PERFECT FRENCH OMELET

Knowing how to make an omelet is a very good skill to have. Filled with leftover grilled or roasted meats or vegetables—or whatever you have on hand—an omelet makes a tasty and quick breakfast, lunch, or dinner. For one omelet, first make the filling of your choice; set aside. Beat 2 eggs, 2 tablespoons water, and freshly ground black pepper to taste in a small bowl until well combined but not frothy. Heat 1 tablespoon olive oil in a small skillet over medium-high heat until skillet is hot (this is crucial to keep the omelet from sticking). Add egg mixture to skillet; reduce heat to medium. Immediately begin stirring eggs gently but consistently until there are small pieces of egg surrounded by liquid egg. Stop stirring. Cook for 30 to 60 seconds or until eggs are set and shiny. Spoon filling across center of omelet. With a spatula, lift and fold an edge of the omelet about one-third of the way toward the center. Fold the opposite edge toward the center. Transfer to a warm plate. Serve immediately.

OMELET FILLINGS

THE DENVER: Cook chopped green and/or red sweet pepper, onion, and basil in olive oil. Stir in leftover chopped grilled pork chop or tenderloin.

SHRIMP-AVOCADO-TOMATO: Combine cooked whole or chopped shrimp, diced avocado, diced tomato, and chopped fresh cilantro.

MIXED MUSHROOM: Cook mixed sliced mushrooms and chopped shallots in olive oil. Stir in chopped fresh chives.

TOMATO-PESTO: Top with chopped tomatoes and Basil Pesto (page 301).

ARGENTINIAN: Top with leftover thinly sliced grilled steak and Chimichurri Sauce (page 305).

SOUTHERN-STYLE: Top with shredded Basic Braised Pork Shoulder (page 92) and BBQ Sauce (page 305).

CHARD-RED ONION: Sauté red onion and chopped Swiss chard (or spinach) in olive oil and garlic. Top omelet with sautéed greens and Paleo Mayo (plain, garlic, or herbed variations, page 305).

MEXICAN: Top with leftover shredded Basic Braised Pork Shoulder (page 92) or cooked ground beef, Chipotle Mayo (page 305), and a mixture of chopped avocado, tomato, onion, cilantro, and minced jalapeño.

SWEET POTATO-PORK: Top with leftover cooked sweet potatoes, leftover cooked pork, and Cilantro Pesto (page 301).

PERFECTLY STEAMED
HARD-COOKED EGGS

MAKES 8 HARD-COOKED EGGS

8 large eggs

This method for hard-cooking eggs results in a creamy but firm yolk that has no green discoloration—a result of overcooking. When the egg is cooked too long, ferrous sulfate forms where the yolk and white meet. Using this method, you'll get beautifully sunny yellow yolks every time. Having a bowl of hard-cooked eggs in the refrigerator is a real boon to the Paleo dieter. They are terrific for breakfast, snacks, and in recipes such as Smoky Chinese Deviled Egg Salad (page 257), and Egg and Veggie Collard Green Salad Wraps (page 258).

Place a steamer basket in a large saucepan; add about 1 inch of water (water should not touch the bottom of the basket). Cover saucepan and bring water to boiling over high heat. Add eggs to the steamer basket. Cook, covered, 12 minutes.

Immediately place eggs in a bowl of ice water for 15 minutes to cool. Peel eggs under cool running water. Store in the refrigerator up to 5 days.

SMOKY CHINESE DEVILED EGG SALAD

>> <<

MAKES 4 SERVINGS

1 teaspoon coconut oil

2 tablespoons minced onion

1 teaspoon salt-free Chinese five-spice powder

1 teaspoon smoked paprika

6 Perfectly Steamed Hard-Cooked Eggs (recipe, page 256), chilled

⅓ cup Paleo Mayo (recipe, page 305)

1 teaspoon salt-free Chinese dry mustard

1 tablespoon minced chives

1 Asian pear, peeled, cored, and finely chopped

½ cup minced celery

½ cup coarsely shredded carrot

8 Bibb lettuce leaves

A mix of spices and spice blends—including Chinese five-spice (equal parts cinnamon, cloves, fennel seeds, star anise, and black pepper), smoked paprika, and dry Chinese mustard—gives this creamy-crunchy egg salad incredible flavor.

In a small saucepan heat coconut oil over medium heat. Add onion; reduce heat to low. Cover and cook 3 minutes or until translucent. Stir in five-spice powder and paprika; cook and stir 30 seconds or until fragrant. Remove onion to a bowl; let cool.

Meanwhile, using the large holes on a box grater, coarsely shred the chilled hard-cooked eggs.

Whisk Paleo Mayo, mustard, and chives into the onion in bowl. Fold in the shredded eggs, pear, celery, and carrot. Serve in lettuce leaves.

EGG AND VEGGIE COLLARD GREEN SALAD WRAPS

>>   <<

MAKES **2** SERVINGS

2   large collard green, Swiss chard, or Bibb lettuce leaves

1   ripe medium avocado, halved, seeded, peeled, and mashed

2   Perfectly Steamed Hard-Cooked Eggs (recipe, page 256), sliced

1   teaspoon Smoky Seasoning (recipe, page 296)

1   small zucchini, shaved into ribbons

8   fresh basil leaves

¼   cup shredded carrot

¼   cup Paleo Aïoli (recipe, page 305)

Use a vegetable peeler to shave the zucchini into ribbons. Just run it down the entire length of the vegetable—all the way around—until you reach the seedy center, which can be discarded.

Remove and discard stems from collard leaves. Using a sharp knife, shave off the tough spine on the back of each leaf (this will make leaves easier to roll).

Place leaves on work surface, top sides up. Spread mashed avocado on a long side of each leaf; layer with eggs, Smoky Seasoning, zucchini, basil, and carrot. Drizzle with 2 tablespoons of the Paleo Aïoli. Roll up; cut crosswise into 1-inch pieces. Serve with the remaining Paleo Aïoli.

Stracciatella with Leeks and
Spinach, *recipe, page 262*

STRACCIATELLA WITH
>> LEEKS AND SPINACH <<

1 lemon
1 medium leek, trimmed and
     thinly sliced
1 tablespoon extra virgin olive oil
2 cloves garlic, minced
6 cups unsalted chicken stock
3 eggs
1 teaspoon Lemon-Herb Seasoning
     (recipe, page 296)
1 6-ounce package fresh baby
     spinach
½ to 1 teaspoon black pepper
½ cup snipped fresh basil
   Lemon wedges

Many cultures enjoy brothy soups that have beaten eggs swirled or dropped into them for both protein and texture (see opposite). Stracciatella [STRAH-cha-TEHL-lah] is the Italian version. "Straccio" is Italian for rag, which refers to the raglike strands the eggs form when dropped into the hot soup.

Remove 1 teaspoon zest and squeeze 1 tablespoon juice from lemon; set lemon zest and juice aside.

In a 4- to 6-quart pot cook leek in olive oil over medium heat about 4 minutes or just until tender. Add garlic; cook and stir 1 minute more. Stir in chicken stock. Bring to boiling. Reduce heat to medium-low.

In a small bowl whisk together the eggs and the Lemon-Herb Seasoning. Gradually add egg mixture while stirring soup in a circular motion to form thin strands of egg. Stir in spinach. Remove pot from heat. Stir in lemon juice, lemon zest, and pepper.

Top servings with basil and serve with lemon wedges.

CHINESE EGG DROP SOUP WITH SHIITAKE MUSHROOMS

>> <<

MAKES 4 SERVINGS

8 cups unsalted chicken stock

¼ cup dry sherry

8 shiitake mushrooms, stems removed and thinly sliced

1 tablespoon minced fresh ginger

1 teaspoon ground white pepper

½ cup water

¼ cup arrowroot

2 tablespoons fresh lemon juice

4 eggs

Thinly sliced scallions

Meaty shiitake mushrooms and eggs give this Asian-style soup enough substance to make a satisfying meal. Serve it with iced green tea.

In a medium saucepan combine stock, sherry, mushrooms, ginger, and white pepper. Bring to boiling; reduce heat to maintain simmer.

In a small bowl whisk together the water and arrowroot until smooth. Add to simmering soup; cook and stir until slightly thickened (soup should coat the back of a spoon). Stir in lemon juice.

In another bowl lightly beat eggs just until yolks and whites are blended. Slowly pour eggs, in a steady stream, into soup while slowly stirring soup. The eggs should cook immediately. Remove saucepan from heat to avoid overcooking eggs. Serve soup topped with scallions.

BALSAMIC ARUGULA SALAD
>> WITH FRIED EGGS AND <<
PORTOBELLO MUSHROOMS

MAKES **4** SERVINGS

½ cup extra virgin olive oil

2 6- to 8-ounce packages sliced
   portobello mushrooms

4 eggs

2 tablespoons balsamic vinegar

1 teaspoon Dijon-Style Mustard
   (recipe, page 304)

½ teaspoon Mediterranean
   Seasoning (recipe, page 296)

1 5- to 6-ounce package arugula

¼ cup unsalted roasted sunflower
   seeds

   Freshly cracked black pepper

Fried or poached eggs served alongside or on top of salad are much loved in many types of cuisines. The best known is a French salad of frisée (French curly endive), lardons (small cubes of bacon), and poached eggs. This Paleo twist on that version features sautéed mushrooms, arugula, and crispy-edged fried eggs.

In a large nonstick skillet heat 2 tablespoons of the olive oil over medium-high heat. Add mushrooms; cook 8 to 10 minutes or until tender and lightly browned, stirring occasionally and adding more oil if needed. Remove mushrooms from skillet. Add 2 tablespoons of the olive oil to the skillet. Fry eggs in hot oil over medium heat until whites are set and yolks are desired doneness, turning if desired.

Meanwhile, whisk together the remaining ¼ cup olive oil, the balsamic vinegar, Dijon-Style Mustard, and Mediterranean Seasoning. In a large bowl drizzle the dressing over the arugula; toss to coat. Serve mushrooms and arugula alongside the fried eggs. Sprinkle sunflower seeds and pepper over mushrooms and salad.

3 WAYS WITH PRECUT PACKAGED KALE

It would be an understatement to say that kale has made inroads into the culinary consciousness of the country in the last few years. Partly because it is so nutritious—it is absolutely packed with vitamins A, C, and K—and partly because creative cooks have discovered all kinds of new ways to use it (think kale chips). Because it is so prevalent in so many recipes, produce companies have come up with ways to make it even more accessible and easy to work into your diet. Kale needs to be well rinsed and dried before chopping—and it should have the tough, fibrous center rib removed. For 30-minute recipes, the washed, precut, and packaged kale now available in produce departments is a real convenience. Try it in Caldo Verde with Poached Eggs (page 267), Open-Face Omelet with Kale, Sweet Peppers, and Butternut Squash (page 268), and Green Garden Smoothie (page 269).

CALDO VERDE WITH POACHED EGGS

>>   <<

MAKES 4 SERVINGS

- 1   cup diced onion
- 1   cup coarsely grated cauliflower
- 2   teaspoons Smoky Seasoning (recipe, page 296)
- 2   tablespoons extra virgin olive oil
- ¼   cup dry sherry or Madeira
- 4   cups unsalted chicken stock
- 3   cups packaged chopped kale
- 1   tablespoon sherry vinegar
- 4   eggs
-     Lemon wedges

There are many versions of this popular Portuguese soup, but the common denominator is kale. Some versions call for collards, but most contain kale. In this Paleo version, grated cauliflower stands in for the puree of white potatoes and the pleasing smoky flavor comes from Smoky Seasoning instead of salty sausage such as linguiça or chorizo.

In a large pot cook onion, cauliflower, and Smoky Seasoning in hot oil over medium heat about 5 minutes or until onion is translucent. Add sherry; cook and stir until nearly evaporated. Add chicken stock and kale. Simmer, uncovered, 2 to 3 minutes or until kale is tender but not mushy. Add vinegar; return soup to simmering.

Crack each egg into its own small ramekin or custard cup. Gently drop the eggs into the simmering soup. Cover and poach to desired doneness, about 4 minutes for soft-set eggs.

Using a slotted spoon, carefully remove each egg from soup and place in a soup bowl. Ladle soup over eggs. Serve immediately with lemon wedges.

OPEN-FACE OMELET WITH
>> KALE, SWEET PEPPERS, <<
AND BUTTERNUT SQUASH

MAKES 4 SERVINGS

2 tablespoons extra virgin olive oil

3 cups packaged chopped kale

1½ cups red, yellow, and/or orange sweet pepper strips

1 cup packaged cubed butternut squash

½ cup thinly sliced red onion

1 tablespoon Mexican Seasoning (recipe, page 296)

⅔ cup unsalted chicken stock

6 eggs

Red wine vinegar

Similar to an Italian frittata—but cooked entirely on the stove-top—this brightly colored egg dish is perfectly doable for a busy morning breakfast or quick weeknight dinner.

Heat oil in a large nonstick skillet over medium-high heat. Add kale, sweet pepper, squash, onion, and Mexican Seasoning; cook and stir about 5 minutes or until onion and peppers begin to soften. Add chicken stock. Cover and cook about 8 minutes or until liquid is nearly evaporated and squash is tender.

In a medium bowl lightly beat eggs. Add eggs to skillet. Cook just until eggs are set and slightly moist on top, pushing the vegetables with a rubber spatula so the uncooked eggs runs underneath. Run the spatula underneath the omelet to prevent it from sticking to the pan.

To serve, cut the omelet into four wedges and drizzle lightly with vinegar.

(3)

>> GREEN GARDEN SMOOTHIE <<

MAKES **2** SERVINGS

2 cups packaged chopped kale

½ of a ripe avocado, cut up

1 medium cucumber, cut into chunks

1 cup carrot juice

½ cup ice cubes

1 2-inch piece of fresh ginger, peeled and cut into chunks

2 tablespoons fresh lime juice

1 mango, seeded, peeled, and cut into chunks

¼ teaspoon Smoky Seasoning (recipe, page 296)

This gorgeous green smoothie gets its beautiful hue and nutrition from kale, avocado, and cucumber—and its flavor from carrot juice, ginger, fresh lime juice, and a surprising pinch of Smoky Seasoning.

In a blender combine all ingredients; process until smooth. Serve immediately.

>> MUSHROOM-SCALLION FRITTATA <<

MAKES 4 SERVINGS

3 tablespoons extra virgin olive oil

1 5-ounce package sliced shiitake
  mushrooms

10 scallions, green and white parts
    cut into 1-inch pieces

1 5-ounce package baby kale,
  arugula, and radicchio blend or
  other greens

¼ cup Classic French Vinaigrette
  (recipe, page 300)

8 eggs

1 teaspoon herbes de Provence
  or Mediterranean Seasoning
  (recipe, page 296)

1 teaspoon lemon zest

¼ teaspoon black pepper

¼ cup snipped fresh parsley

  Lemon wedges

Herbes de Provence is a traditional blend of dried herbs used in abundance in the cooking of southern France. The mixture usually contains some combination of basil, fennel seeds, lavender, marjoram, rosemary, sage, summer savory, and thyme. If you don't have it on hand, Mediterranean Seasoning is a good substitute.

Preheat broiler. In a large broilerproof skillet heat oil over medium heat; add mushrooms and scallions. Cover and cook 10 minutes or until tender.

Meanwhile, place greens in a large bowl. Drizzle with Classic French Vinaigrette; toss to coat.

In a medium bowl whisk together eggs, herbes de Provence, lemon zest, and pepper. Pour eggs into skillet over mushrooms and scallions. Cook over medium heat. As eggs set, run a spatula around edge of skillet, lifting eggs so the uncooked portion flows underneath.

Place skillet under broiler 4 to 5 inches from heat. Broil 1 to 2 minutes or just until top is set and golden brown. Sprinkle with parsley.

Cut frittata into wedges and serve with tossed greens and lemon wedges.

SWEET POTATO-
>> MUSHROOM PANCAKES WITH <<
SPICY SKILLET SPINACH

MAKES **4** SERVINGS

8 eggs, lightly beaten

1 pound sweet potatoes, peeled
   and finely shredded

1 cup thinly sliced cremini
   mushrooms

½ cup thinly sliced scallions

¼ cup almond flour

1 teaspoon Smoky Seasoning
   (recipe, page 296)

3 cloves garlic, minced

6 tablespoons extra virgin olive oil

½ teaspoon crushed red pepper

1 5- to 6-ounce package fresh
   baby spinach

   Lemon wedges

Keep the cooked pancakes warm on a paper towel-lined rimmed baking sheet in a 200°F oven while you finish cooking the pancakes and sauté the spinach.

For batter, in a medium bowl stir together eggs, sweet potatoes, mushrooms, scallions, almond flour, Smoky Seasoning, and 1 of the minced garlic cloves.

Heat a griddle or an extra-large skillet over medium-high heat. Brush the surface with some of the olive oil. For each pancake, pour ¼ cup of the batter onto the hot griddle. Cook 2 to 3 minutes or until the bottoms are golden. Turn pancakes; cook 1 to 2 minutes more or until second sides are golden. Repeat with the remaining batter, adding more oil as necessary.

In a large skillet heat 2 tablespoons of the olive oil over medium heat. Add the remaining 2 minced garlic cloves and the crushed red pepper. Cook and stir 1 minute. Add the spinach; cook 2 minutes or just until spinach wilts, stirring occasionally. Serve pancakes with spinach and lemon wedges.

POACHED EGGS WITH
>> GRILLED SCALLIONS, ASPARAGUS, << AND SALSA VERDE

MAKES **6** SERVINGS

1 lemon

1½ cups lightly packed parsley leaves, chopped

½ cup extra virgin olive oil

1 tablespoon finely minced red onion

1 clove garlic, minced

1 teaspoon smoked paprika

½ teaspoon freshly ground black pepper

2 teaspoons sherry vinegar or white wine vinegar

1 pound thin asparagus spears

8 scallions

6 eggs

If you are hesitant to poach eggs, take heart: This muffin-cup method turns out perfect poached eggs every time. Be sure to oil the cups generously to ensure that the eggs will pop right out of the pan.

For the salsa verde, remove 2 teaspoons zest and squeeze 3 tablespoons juice from lemon. In a medium bowl combine the lemon zest and juice, parsley, ¼ cup of the olive oil, the onion, garlic, paprika, and pepper. Set aside to let flavors blend.

Snap off and discard woody bases from asparagus. Trim ends from scallions. Drizzle asparagus and scallions with the remaining ¼ cup olive oil, turning vegetables to coat. Grill vegetables over medium-high heat 6 to 7 minutes or until nicely charred and crisp-tender, turning once. Remove vegetables from grill. (Or cook vegetables on a stove-top grill pan over medium-high heat.)

For the poached eggs, lightly brush the sides and bottoms of six muffin cups with additional olive oil. Pour 1½ to 2 cups water into an extra-large skillet with a tight-fitting lid (skillet should be large enough to accommodate muffin pan and the water should come halfway up sides of muffin pan). Bring water to a simmer.

Meanwhile, carefully crack an egg into each oiled muffin cup. Place muffin pan in the simmering water and cover tightly. Cook, without lifting the lid, until the whites are set and yolks are desired doneness (about 4 minutes for soft yolks).

Carefully remove muffin pan from water. Place muffin pan on a kitchen towel; pat pan with towel to dry. Place a platter or baking sheet over the pan and gently invert it to release eggs. Serve eggs on the grilled vegetables and drizzle with salsa verde.

>> THAI-STYLE FRIED RICE <<

MAKES **4** SERVINGS

4   cups purchased fresh cauliflower
    florets

4   tablespoons coconut oil

1   8-ounce package sliced fresh
    button mushrooms

¾   cup coarsely chopped scallions

½   cup purchased shredded carrots

½   cup diced cooked pork

1   tablespoon minced fresh ginger

4   cloves garlic, minced

½   teaspoon black pepper

6   eggs

1   lime

½   teaspoon crushed red pepper
    (optional)

⅓   cup chopped fresh basil

⅓   cup chopped fresh cilantro

    Lime wedges

As is typical in traditional foods that have been converted to be Paleo-compliant, the "rice" in this Thai-style dish is finely chopped cauliflower, making this take-out favorite simple to do at home—and in line with a healthful diet.

In a food processor pulse cauliflower (in batches if necessary) until the pieces are the size of rice. In an extra-large skillet cook cauliflower rice in 2 tablespoons of the oil 5 minutes or until tender and just beginning to brown, stirring occasionally. Remove to a large bowl.

In the same skillet cook mushrooms, scallions, and carrots over medium-high heat 4 minutes or until crisp-tender. Add pork, ginger, garlic, and black pepper; cook and stir 1 minute. Push vegetables and pork to the side of skillet to make a well in the center. Add the remaining 2 tablespoons oil to center of skillet. Crack eggs into center; break the yolks. Cook until eggs are set but still slightly wet. Using a spatula, roughly chop eggs.

Push vegetables back into center and fold into eggs. Fold in cauliflower rice. Remove 1½ teaspoons zest and 2 tablespoons juice from lime. Add lime zest and juice and, if desired, crushed red pepper to fried rice. Sprinkle with basil and cilantro. Serve with lime wedges.

PORTOBELLOS WITH POACHED EGGS AND SWEET PEPPER SAUTÉ

>>   <<

MAKES 2 SERVINGS

- 1 16-ounce package red, yellow, orange, and/or green sweet pepper strips
- 3 tablespoons extra virgin olive oil
- 2 cloves garlic, minced
   Coarsely ground black pepper
- 2 cups baby spinach leaves
- 4 sun-dried tomatoes, diced
- 4 portobello mushrooms, stemmed
- ½ teaspoon garlic powder
- 8 cups water
- ¼ cup apple cider or white vinegar
- 4 eggs
- 2 tablespoons chopped fresh basil

The gills of portobello mushrooms are perfectly fine to eat, but when they're cooked, they turn anything they touch black. If you're not eating them whole—grilled, for instance—it's not a bad idea to scrape them out. And in this recipe, you need the space to accommodate the spinach, dried tomatoes, and poached eggs.

Preheat broiler. Line a large rimmed baking sheet with foil.

In an extra-large skillet cook sweet peppers in 1 tablespoon hot olive oil 6 minutes or until crisp-tender, adding minced garlic after about 3 minutes. Season with black pepper. Remove from skillet; keep warm. In the same skillet cook spinach and dried tomatoes in 1 tablespoon hot oil 1 minute or just until wilted. Keep warm. Wipe out skillet.

Meanwhile, scrape gills from caps. Brush both sides of mushroom caps with remaining 1 tablespoon olive oil. Place on baking sheet, stems sides down, and broil on the middle oven rack 3 to 4 minutes or just until tender. Remove from the oven; sprinkle inside of caps with garlic powder.

While mushroom caps are broiling, add the water and vinegar to the skillet.* Bring to boiling; reduce heat to simmer. Break an egg into a custard cup or ramekin and slip egg into simmering water. Repeat with remaining eggs. Simmer, uncovered, 3 to 5 minutes or until whites are completely set and yolks begin to thicken but are not hard. Transfer eggs to a double thickness of paper towels to drain.

Top each mushroom cap with some of the spinach-dried tomato mixture; top with a poached egg. Sprinkle with black pepper and top with basil. Serve with sweet peppers.

*Use 1 tablespoon vinegar per 2 cups water.

>> SWEET POTATO PYTT I PANNA <<

MAKES 4 SERVINGS

1 8.8-ounce package refrigerated cooked beets, thinly sliced

6 tablespoons balsamic vinegar

4 tablespoons extra virgin olive oil

2 cups diced sweet potatoes

2 cups diced cooked beef, lamb, or pork

1 cup diced sweet onion

¼ teaspoon black pepper

1 tablespoon Dijon-Style Mustard (recipe, page 304)

1 tablespoon snipped fresh thyme

1 tablespoon snipped fresh rosemary (optional)

4 eggs

"Pytt i panna" means "small pieces in pan" in Swedish, which refers to the chopped-up bits of leftover meats and vegetables that make up this dish (think Swedish hash). Traditionally, it's served topped with a fried egg and pickled beets and cornichons on the side. Use an extra-large skillet so that the pieces get browned and crispy. Using too small a pan results in steaming the mixture, which turns it to mush.

In a small bowl combine beets and 4 tablespoons of the vinegar. Set aside.

In an extra-large skillet heat 2 tablespoons of the oil over medium heat. Add sweet potatoes, spreading in an even layer. Cook 10 minutes or just until potatoes are tender and beginning to brown. Add cooked meat, onion, and pepper; cook 5 minutes or until onions are tender and golden brown. Add the remaining 2 tablespoons vinegar, the Dijon-Style Mustard, thyme, and, if desired, rosemary.

Meanwhile, in a large skillet heat the remaining 2 tablespoons oil over medium heat. Break eggs into skillet. Reduce heat to low; fry eggs 2 minutes or until whites are set and yolks are desired doneness.

To serve, divide hash and beets among four plates. Top with fried eggs.

*Tip: For cooked beef, see Basic Roast Beef, page 34. For cooked pork, see Basic Braised Pork Shoulder, page 92.

>> MATCHA SMOOTHIE <<

1 cup fresh orange juice

1 cup unsweetened almond milk

1 frozen banana, cut into chunks

1 to 2 teaspoons matcha

1 cup ice

Matcha is a gorgeously green-hued powder made from dried and ground green tea leaves. (It's the featured tea in Japanese tea ceremonies.) When you drink green tea steeped from leaves, you are drinking water with the essence of tea in it. When you drink matcha, you are drinking the whole leaf. It is very high in antioxidants. In fact, you would have to drink 10 cups of green tea steeped from leaves to get the same amount of antioxidants in a single cup of matcha.

In a blender combine all ingredients. Blend until smooth. Serve immediately.

>> RAITA-STYLE SMOOTHIE <<

MAKES 2 SERVINGS

½ of a cucumber, seeded and cut
  into chunks

1 10-ounce bag frozen pineapple
  chunks

⅓ cup fresh mint

1 jalapeño chile, halved and seeded
  (tip, page 37)

2 cups unsweetened almond milk

1 cup ice

½ teaspoon cumin seeds, toasted
  (tip, page 69)

1 tablespoon snipped cilantro

Raita is an Indian yogurt-based condiment flavored with mint, coriander, and cumin. It's served with a meal to cool the heat of fiery curries and chutneys. This refreshing smoothie uses the same flavor elements.

In a blender combine cucumber, pineapple, mint, and jalapeño. Add almond milk and ice; blend until smooth.

Pour smoothie into two glasses. Top with cumin seeds and cilantro. Serve immediately.

Caprese Smoothie,
recipe, page 284

>> CAPRESE SMOOTHIE <<

MAKES 2 SERVINGS

6 ripe roma tomatoes, halved, or
  2 cups sweet grape or cherry
  tomatoes

1 fennel bulb, trimmed and sliced

1 cup chilled unsalted vegetable
  stock

1 lemon, peeled and seeds
  removed

1 cup ice

2 tablespoons Basil Pesto (recipe,
  page 301)

This light and fresh smoothie is perfect for a hot summer night, when you need a pick-me-up but don't want a heavy meal. Caprese is a simple and traditional Italian salad of ripe tomato and fresh mozzarella topped with basil and olive oil. This inspired smoothie has all the flavors of that salad without the dairy that can cause digestive issues and inflammation.

In a blender combine the tomatoes, fennel, vegetable stock, lemon, and ice. Blend until smooth.

Pour into two glasses. Top each with 1 tablespoon Basil Pesto and swirl into smoothie.

>> PUMPKIN PIE SMOOTHIE <<

MAKES **2** SERVINGS

½ of a 15-ounce can pumpkin

1 cup unsweetened almond milk

1 orange, peeled and sectioned
   (tip, page 114)

½ cup chopped red apple

¼ cup frozen unsweetened pitted
   sweet cherries

2 tablespoons hemp seed hearts or
   flaxseed meal

1 teaspoon pumpkin pie spice

½ teaspoon vanilla

One cup of mashed, cooked, pumpkin contains more than double the recommended daily intake of vitamin A, which has been shown to improve eye health. Hemp seed hearts have a deliciously nutty taste and are one of the most dense sources of plant proteins, which make them a wonderful addition to whole-meal smoothies—when animal protein is not part of the equation.

Combine all ingredients in a blender. Blend until smooth.

SWEET CHERRY-ALMOND FLAXSEED SMOOTHIE

MAKES 2 SERVINGS

2 cups frozen unsweetened pitted sweet cherries

½ cup fresh orange juice

½ cup unsweetened almond milk

¼ cup ground almonds

2 tablespoons flaxseed meal

½ teaspoon almond extract

Chopped almonds (optional)

Flaxseed is a complete protein source—which means it contains every amino acid your body doesn't make on its own. It adds both body and protein to this pretty pink smoothie. If you like, top the smoothies with chopped almonds for a bit of crunch.

Combine all ingredients in a blender. Blend until smooth.

Pour into two glasses. If desired, top with chopped almonds.

>> RUBY RED SMOOTHIE <<

2 packaged baby beets (about
   8 ounces), peeled and cut
   into chunks

2 medium carrots, cut into chunks

1 navel orange, peeled

1 Granny Smith apple, cored and
   sliced

1 cup ice

1 cup fresh orange juice

Beets are on everyone's list of superfoods and for good reason: High in vitamins and minerals, they also cleanse the body, contain betaine and tryptophan to boost your mental health, and are a high source of energy. Carrots, an orange, an apple, and a little fresh orange juice add a touch of sweetness in this gorgeous smoothie.

Combine all ingredients in a blender.* Blend until smooth.

*Tip: A high-powered blender, such as a Vitamix, yields a smoothie with a creamy, silky texture. If you only have a regular blender, you can still make smoothies, but the texture will not be as smooth. If you make Ruby Red Smoothie in a regular blender, be sure to use packaged beets. If you opt for raw beets, you will need the high-powered blender.

BLACKBERRY-GINGER-COCONUT MILK SMOOTHIE

>> <<

MAKES 2 SERVINGS

2 cups frozen blackberries

½ inch piece of fresh ginger, peeled

1 cup canned coconut milk (see headnote)

½ cup fresh orange juice

2 tablespoons hemp seed hearts or flaxseed meal

Shredded coconut, toasted (tip, page 159)

Be sure to thoroughly mix the coconut milk (or vigorously shake the can) before measuring in order to incorporate the coconut cream that rises to the top with the rest of the liquid.

In a blender combine blackberries, ginger, coconut milk, orange juice, and hemp seed hearts or flaxseed meal. Blend until smooth.

Pour into two glasses and top with toasted coconut.

CREAMY CHOCOLATE-
ALMOND SMOOTHIE

\>\>   \<\<

14 pitted unsweetened, unsulfured
   whole dates

 1 cup boiling water

 1 large avocado

 2 medium bananas

 2 cups unsweetened almond milk

⅓ cup unsweetened cocoa powder

¼ cup no salt added almond butter

 1 teaspoon vanilla

1½ cups ice*

 1 tablespoon egg white powder

This rich, chocolaty smoothie may taste like dessert, but it is sugar- and dairy-free and is packed with all kinds of nutritionally good things—dates, avocado, banana, and a shot of protein from almond butter and egg white powder.

In a 2-cup glass measuring cup combine the dates and the boiling water. Let stand 10 minutes.

Meanwhile, halve and seed avocado. Scoop the avocado flesh from the peel and place in a blender. Peel bananas; cut in half and add to blender. Add almond milk, cocoa powder, almond butter, vanilla, and the undrained dates. Blend until smooth, stopping to scrape sides as needed. Add ice; blend until smooth. Add egg white powder; cover and blend just until combined.

*Tip: Add more ice for a thinner consistency and to make smoothies colder.

PALEO
PANTRY

This collection of spice blends, salad dressings and vinaigrettes, and condiments is a big part of the magic of the great flavors in this book. None of them has any salt, additives, or other non-Paleo ingredients. Spend a little time on the weekend preparing your most often-used pantry items, and even on the busiest weeknights, meal prep will be a breeze.

STOCKING YOUR PALEO PANTRY

Because much of the success of The Paleo Diet hinges on its exclusion of processed foods and its inclusion of fresh, whole, living foods, the Paleo convert can't just stop by the supermarket and pick up a frozen dinner in a bag and call it a day—that's what got us in a lot of dietary and health trouble in the first place. The truth is that in order to eat preservative- and salt-free foods, you will need to make some—but not all—of the staples that are the backbone and flavoring agents of the recipes in this book.

As I've mentioned, salt-free tomato products, beef and chicken stocks, and even some spice blends are readily available. But certain products—condiments such as ketchup, mayonnaise, and mustard; sauces such as BBQ and pesto; and salad dressings and vinaigrettes will need to be made fresh by you. None of these recipes— all contained in the following page—takes much time or is particularly difficult. With a little planning, you can make up the most commonly used pantry items on the weekend—or whenever you have a window of time—and store them for use during the week. Check out the storage methods and times for each recipe. Many of them, like pesto, can be frozen for long-term storage.

Check out the list of absolute essentials, opposite. With these items on your shelf, in the fridge, or in the freezer, you will be ready to cook a perfect Paleo dinner any night of the week.

IN THE PANTRY

- Salt-free spice blends
- Ground black pepper
- Dried herbs
- Ground spices
- Salt-free chicken stock
- Salt-free beef stock
- Salt-free tomato paste
- Salt-free tomatoes (crushed, diced regular, and fire-roasted)
- Almond flour
- Coconut flour
- Flaxseed meal
- Arrowroot powder
- Dry white wine
- Dry red wine
- Extra virgin olive oil
- Coconut oil
- Canned coconut milk
- Coconut milk
- Red white vinegar
- Balsamic vinegar
- White wine vinegar
- Whole unroasted, unsalted cashews
- Whole unroasted, unsalted almonds
- Whole unroasted, unsalted walnuts
- Sesame seeds
- Dried apricots (unsulfured)
- Dates (unsweetened)
- Raisins (unsulfured)
- Dried cherries (unsweetened or naturally sweetened and unsulfured)
- Dried cranberries (unsweetened or naturally sweetened and unsulfured)
- Canned no-salt-added tuna

IN COOL STORAGE

- Garlic
- Onions
- Shallots
- Sweet potatoes

IN THE REFRIGERATOR

- Eggs
- Almond milk
- Paleo Ketchup
- Paleo Mayonnaise
- Paleo Mustard
- Lemons
- Limes
- Oranges
- Scallions
- Fresh gingerroot
- Paleo salad dressing(s)
- Fresh herbs
- Lettuces/salad greens

IN THE FREEZER

- Pesto
- BBQ Sauce
- Chimichurri Sauce
- Frozen fruits
- Frozen vegetables (blends and single varieties)

>> SEASONING BLENDS <<

Making your own seasoning blends ensures that they will be salt- and preservative-free—and they taste so much fresher than store-bought blends. These aromatic mixtures are versatile and offer a wide range of flavors for a variety of applications.

LEMON-HERB SEASONING

- 6 tablespoons dried lemon peel
- 1 tablespoon herbes de Provence
- 2 teaspoons onion powder
- 1 teaspoon black pepper

In a small bowl combine lemon peel, herbes de Provence, onion powder, and pepper. Store in an airtight container at room temperature up to 6 months. Stir or shake before using. Makes about ½ cup.

MEDITERRANEAN SEASONING

- 2 teaspoons fennel seeds
- 1 teaspoon dried rosemary
- 1 tablespoon dried oregano
- 1 tablespoon dried thyme
- 2 teaspoons preservative-free granulated garlic
- 1 teaspoon dried lemon peel

In a dry small skillet toast fennel seeds over medium-low heat 1 to 2 minutes or until fragrant, shaking skillet occasionally. Remove from heat; cool 2 minutes. Transfer seeds to a spice grinder; grind to a powder. Add rosemary; grind until rosemary is coarsely ground. Transfer fennel and rosemary to a small bowl. Stir in oregano, thyme, garlic, and lemon peel. Store in an airtight container at room temperature up to 6 months. Stir or shake before using. Makes about ⅓ cup.

MEXICAN SEASONING

- 1 tablespoon cumin seeds
- 4 teaspoons paprika
- 1 tablespoon preservative-free granulated garlic
- 1 teaspoon dried oregano
- ½ to 1 teaspoon ground chipotle pepper or cayenne pepper (optional)
- ½ teaspoon ground cinnamon
- ¼ teaspoon ground saffron

In a dry small skillet toast cumin seeds over medium-low heat 1 to 2 minutes or until fragrant, shaking skillet occasionally. Remove from heat; cool 2 minutes. Transfer seeds to a spice grinder; grind to a powder. Transfer cumin to a small bowl. Stir in paprika, garlic, oregano, chipotle pepper (if using), cinnamon, and saffron. Store in an airtight container at room temperature up to 6 months. Stir or shake before using. Makes about ¼ cup.

SMOKY SEASONING

- ¼ cup smoked paprika
- 4 teaspoons dried orange peel
- 2 teaspoons garlic powder
- 1 teaspoon onion powder
- 1 teaspoon ground cloves
- 1 teaspoon dried basil

In a small bowl combine smoked paprika, orange peel, garlic powder, onion powder, cloves, and dried basil. Store in an airtight container at room temperature up to 6 months. Stir or shake before using. Makes about ½ cup.

CAJUN SEASONING

- 2 tablespoons paprika
- 1 tablespoon garlic powder
- 1 tablespoon onion powder
- 2 teaspoons dried thyme, crushed
- 2 teaspoons white pepper
- 1½ teaspoons black pepper
- 1 teaspoon cayenne pepper
- 1 teaspoon dried oregano, crushed

In a small bowl combine paprika, garlic powder, onion powder, thyme, white pepper, black pepper, cayenne pepper, and oregano. Store in an airtight container up to 6 months. Stir or shake before using. Makes about ⅓ cup.

JAMAICAN JERK SEASONING

- 1 tablespoon onion powder
- 1 tablespoon dried thyme, crushed
- 1½ teaspoons ground allspice
- 1 teaspoon black pepper
- ½ teaspoon ground nutmeg
- ½ teaspoon ground cinnamon
- ½ teaspoon ground cloves
- ¼ teaspoon cayenne pepper

In a small bowl stir together onion powder, thyme, allspice, black pepper, nutmeg, cinnamon, cloves, and cayenne pepper. Store in an airtight container in a cool, dry place up to 6 months. Stir or shake before using. Makes about ¼ cup.

Jamaican Jerk
Seasoning

Smoky
Seasoning

Lemon-Herb
Seasoning

Mexican
Seasoning

Mediterranean
Seasoning

Cajun
Seasoning

*Bright Citrus Vinaigrette,
recipe, page 300*

>> SALAD DRESSINGS <<

Tossing a big salad and grilling a piece of meat is one of the simplest ways to eat Paleo. But bottled dressings rely on a whole host of artificial ingredients for their flavor, body, and long shelf life. The following homemade dressings are all about freshness and flavor. Store any leftovers in the refrigerator up to 3 days—or use a vinaigrette as a marinade.

BRIGHT CITRUS VINAIGRETTE

- ¼ cup minced shallots
- 2 teaspoons orange zest
- 2 teaspoons lemon zest
- 2 teaspoons lime zest
- ½ cup fresh orange juice
- ¼ cup fresh lemon juice
- ¼ cup fresh lime juice
- 2 tablespoons Dijon-Style Mustard (recipe, page 304) or 1 teaspoon dry mustard
- ⅔ cup extra virgin olive oil
- ¼ cup finely snipped fresh parsley, chives, tarragon, or basil
- ½ to 1 teaspoon black pepper

In a medium bowl whisk together shallots, citrus zest, citrus juices, and Dijon-Style Mustard; let stand 3 minutes. Slowly whisk in the olive oil until emulsified. Stir in herb and pepper. Makes about 2 cups.

CLASSIC FRENCH VINAIGRETTE

- 6 tablespoons fresh lemon juice
- 3 shallots, minced
- 1½ tablespoons Dijon-Style Mustard (recipe, page 304)
- 1 cup extra virgin olive oil
- 1 tablespoon finely snipped chives (optional)
- 1 tablespoon finely snipped Italian parsley (optional)
- 2 teaspoons finely snipped fresh tarragon (optional)

In a medium bowl combine lemon juice and shallots. Let stand 15 minutes.

Whisk in Dijon-Style Mustard. Slowly whisk in olive oil in a very thin stream until mixture thickens and emulsifies. Taste vinaigrette. If it is too sharp, whisk in additional Dijon-Style Mustard or olive oil as desired.

If desired, before serving, whisk in herbs. When dressing salad greens with vinaigrette, add freshly cracked black pepper to the bowl and toss to coat. Store vinaigrette in a tightly covered container in the refrigerator up to 1 week. Makes about 1 ¼ cups.

MANGO-LIME SALAD DRESSING

- 1 small ripe mango, peeled, pitted, and coarsely chopped
- 3 tablespoons walnut or coconut oil
- 1 teaspoon lime zest
- 2 tablespoons fresh lime juice
- 2 teaspoons grated fresh ginger
   Dash cayenne pepper
- 1 tablespoon water (optional)

In a food processor or blender combine mango, walnut oil, lime zest, lime juice, ginger, and cayenne pepper. Cover and process or blend until smooth. If needed, thin dressing with the water to desired consistency. Cover and store up to 1 week in the refrigerator. If using coconut oil, bring dressing to room temperature before using. Makes about 1 cup.

ROASTED GARLIC VINAIGRETTE

- 1 medium bulb garlic
- ¾ cup extra virgin olive oil
- ¼ cup fresh lemon juice
- 1 teaspoon dried Greek oregano, crushed

Preheat oven to 400°F. Cut ¼ inch from top of garlic bulb; drizzle with 1 teaspoon of the oil. Wrap in foil. Roast 30 to 35 minutes or until garlic is golden brown and very soft. Cool; squeeze cloves from the bulb into a bowl. Mash into a paste. In a bowl combine lemon juice and oregano. Let stand 5 minutes. Whisk in remaining oil. Whisk in garlic paste. Let stand at room temperature 2 hours before using or refrigerating. Store in refrigerator up to 1 week. Makes about 1 ¼ cups.

MACADAMIA NUT DRESSING

- 4 ounces macadamia nuts, toasted
- 1 teaspoon extra virgin olive oil
- 6 tablespoons water
- ¼ cup fresh lemon juice
- 1 clove garlic, minced
- ¼ teaspoon smoked paprika
- ⅛ teaspoon cayenne pepper

In a blender or food processor combine macadamia nuts and oil. Cover and blend or process until smooth. Add the water, lemon juice, garlic, paprika, and cayenne pepper. Cover and blend or process until smooth. Makes about 1 cup.

>> PESTOS <<

As you will note from browsing the recipes in this book, these fresh pestos can be used in a multitude of ways. Use them to top a grilled steak, toss with roasted vegetables, and stir into Paleo Mayo (page 305) for a spread or dip. Each one has its own unique flavor. One features peppery arugula, walnuts, and lemon. Another combines the earthy flavor of cilantro with the sweetness of pecans and orange. And the classic is a blend of sweet basil, parsley, almonds, and garlic.

ARUGULA PESTO

- 2 cups tightly packed arugula leaves
- 1/3 cup walnuts, toasted*
- 1 tablespoon lemon zest (from 2 lemons)
- 1 clove garlic
- 1/2 cup walnut oil
- 1/4 to 1/2 teaspoon black pepper

In a food processor combine arugula, walnuts, lemon zest, and garlic. Pulse until coarsely chopped. With the processor running, pour the walnut oil in a thin stream into the bowl. Season with pepper.

Use immediately or divide into desired portions and freeze up to 3 months in tightly covered containers. Makes ¾ cup.

*TIP: To toast nuts, spread in a single layer on a rimmed baking sheet. Bake in a 375°F oven 5 to 10 minutes or until lightly toasted, stirring nuts or shaking pan once or twice. Let cool completely before using.

BASIL PESTO

- 2 cups packed fresh basil leaves
- 1 cup packed fresh parsley
- 3 cloves garlic
- 1/2 cup almonds, toasted (tip, below left)
- 1 cup extra virgin olive oil
- 1/4 teaspoon freshly ground black pepper

In a food processor combine basil, parsley, garlic, and almonds. Pulse until coarsely chopped. With the processor running, pour the olive oil in a thin stream into the bowl. Add pepper.

Use immediately or freeze in desired portions up to 3 months in tightly covered containers. Makes 1 ½ cups.

CILANTRO PESTO

- 2 cups lightly packed fresh cilantro leaves
- 1/3 cup pecan halves, toasted (tip, below left)
- 1 tablespoon orange zest (from 1 large orange)
- 1 clove garlic
- 1/2 cup avocado oil
- 1/8 teaspoon cayenne pepper

In a food processor combine cilantro, pecans, orange zest, and garlic. Pulse until coarsely chopped. With the processor running, pour the avocado oil in a thin stream into the bowl. Add cayenne pepper.

Use immediately or freeze in desired portions up to 3 months in tightly covered containers. Makes ¾ cup.

Basil Pesto, recipe, page 301

>> CONDIMENTS <<

We're very fond of a few favorite condiments—ketchup, mustard, mayonnaise, and BBQ sauce. They are used generously on their own as spreads and dips, but they are also crucial elements in recipes as flavoring agents and binders. Commercially produced condiments are loaded with salt, sugar, and preservatives, but these fresh and unadulterated homemade versions are perfectly Paleo and full of flavor. Cashew Cream is a rich, velvety mixture that makes a great stand-in for dairy sour cream, cream, and yogurt.

CASHEW CREAM

1   cup raw cashews

Rinse cashews; drain and place in a bowl or jar. Add enough water to cover by about 1 inch. Cover and let stand at room temperature at least 4 hours and preferably overnight.

Drain cashews; rinse under cold water. Place cashews in a high-power blender* and add ¾ cup of water; process until smooth, scraping down the sides. Add additional water, 1 tablespoon at a time, to reach desired consistency.

Store cashew cream in an airtight container in the refrigerator up to 1 week. Makes about 2 cups.

*NOTE: You may use a regular blender and process on high; the texture of the cream will not be as smooth.

PALEO KETCHUP

½   cup raisins
1   28-ounce can no-salt-added tomato puree
½   cup cider vinegar
1   small onion, chopped
1   clove garlic, chopped
¼   teaspoon ground allspice
¼   teaspoon ground cinnamon
⅛   teaspoon ground mace
⅛   teaspoon ground cloves
⅛   teaspoon cayenne pepper
⅛   teaspoon black pepper

In a small bowl cover raisins with boiling water. Let stand 10 minutes; drain.

In a medium saucepan combine raisins, tomato puree, vinegar, onion, garlic, allspice, cinnamon, mace, cloves, cayenne pepper, and black pepper. Bring to boiling; reduce heat. Simmer, uncovered, 20 to 25 minutes or until onion is tender, stirring frequently to keep mixture from burning. (Be careful; mixture will spatter as it cooks.)

Remove from heat. Let cool about 30 minutes or until just slightly warm. Transfer to a high-power blender* or food processor. Cover and process or blend to desired consistency.

Divide between two clean pint glass jars. Use immediately or freeze up to 2 months. Store in refrigerator up to 1 month. Makes about 3½ cups.

*NOTE: You can use a regular blender, but the consistency won't be as smooth.

DIJON-STYLE MUSTARD

¾   cup brown mustard seeds
¾   cup unsweetened apple juice or cider
¼   cup white wine vinegar
¼   cup dry white wine or water
½   teaspoon turmeric
1   to 2 tablespoons water

In a glass bowl stir together mustard seeds, apple juice, vinegar, wine, and turmeric. Cover tightly and let stand at room temperature 48 hours.

Transfer mixture to a high-powered blender.* Cover and blend until smooth, adding enough of the water to make desired consistency. If air bubbles form, stop and stir mixture. For a smoother texture, press the finished mustard through a fine-mesh sieve.

Use immediately or store in the refrigerator in a tightly covered container up to 1 month. (The flavor will mellow with storage.) Makes about 1¾ cups.

*NOTE: You may use a regular blender and process on high speed; the texture of the mustard will not be as smooth.

BBQ SAUCE

2 pounds ripe roma tomatoes, quartered lengthwise and seeded
1 large sweet onion, cut into thin wedges
1 red sweet pepper, halved and seeded
2 poblano chiles, halved and seeded (tip, page 37)
2 teaspoons Smoky Seasoning (recipe, page 296)
2 tablespoons extra virgin olive oil
½ cup fresh orange juice
⅓ cup raisins
3 tablespoons cider vinegar
2 tablespoons no-salt-added tomato paste
1 tablespoon minced garlic
⅛ teaspoon ground cloves

In an extra-large bowl combine tomatoes, onion, sweet pepper, poblano chiles, Smoky Seasoning, and olive oil. Grill, covered, over medium heat for 20 to 25 minutes or until very tender and charred, stirring occasionally; remove from grill and cool slightly.

In a small saucepan heat orange juice until simmering. Remove saucepan from heat and add the raisins; let stand 10 minutes.

In a food processor or blender combine the grilled vegetables, raisins and juice, vinegar, tomato paste, garlic, and cloves. Cover and process or blend until very smooth, scraping sides as needed. Transfer vegetable mixture to a large saucepan. Bring to simmering; cook to desired consistency. Cool. Use immediately or transfer to clean pint jars and freeze up to 2 months. Makes about 4 cups.

CHIMICHURRI SAUCE

2 cups lightly packed fresh Italian parsley
2 cups lightly packed cilantro
½ cup lightly packed mint
½ cup chopped shallots
1 tablespoon minced garlic (6 cloves)
⅓ cup red wine vinegar
2 dried unsulfured apricots, finely chopped
⅛ teaspoon crushed red pepper
¾ cup extra virgin olive oil

In a food processor or blender combine all ingredients. Process until ingredients are finely chopped and combined, scraping sides as necessary. Use immediately or freeze in desired portions up to 3 months in tightly covered containers. Makes about 2 cups.

PALEO MAYO

1 large or extra-large egg, room temperature
1 tablespoon fresh lemon juice or white wine vinegar
½ teaspoon dry mustard
1 cup walnut, avocado, or extra virgin olive oil, at room temperature*

Crack egg into a tall, narrow glass jar (a wide-mouth pint canning jar works well). Add lemon juice and dry mustard.

Carefully pour in oil. Let egg settle down to the bottom of the jar, under the oil.

Insert an immersion blender and push it all of the way to the bottom of the jar. Turn power on high and let it run for 20 seconds without moving it. The mayonnaise will start to form and rise to the top of the jar. Slowly raise the blender until it reaches the top of the jar. Use mayonnaise immediately or store in the refrigerator up to 1 week. Makes about 3½ cups.

PALEO AÏOLI (GARLIC MAYO): Add 1 clove minced garlic with lemon juice and mustard in Step 2.

HERBED PALEO MAYO: Fold 2 tablespoons snipped fresh herbs into finished mayonnaise. Good choices include chives, parsley, tarragon, and basil—solo or in any combination.

WASABI PALEO MAYO: Add 1 teaspoon all-natural, preservative-free wasabi powder with the lemon juice and mustard in Step 2.

CHIPOTLE PALEO MAYO: Add 2 to 3 teaspoons ground chipotle chile pepper with lemon juice and mustard.

*NOTE: If you use extra virgin olive oil, the olive flavor will come through in the mayonnaise. For a milder flavor, use walnut or avocado oil.

Paleo Ketchup, *recipe, page 304*

Herbed Paleo Mayo, *recipe, page 305*

Dijon-Style Mustard, *recipe, page 304*

>> INDEX <<